CULTURES OF THE WORLD
Bulgaria

Cavendish
Square

New York

Published in 2017 by Cavendish Square Publishing, LLC
243 5th Avenue, Suite 136, New York, NY 10016
Copyright © 2017 by Cavendish Square Publishing, LLC

Third Edition

Library of Congress Cataloging-in-Publication Data

Names: Stavreva, Kirilka, author. | Quek, Lynette, author. | Mattern, Joanne, 1963- author.
Title: Bulgaria / Kirilka Stavreva, Lynette Quek, and Joanne Mattern.
Description: New York : Cavendish Square Publishing, 2017. | Series: Cultures of the world | Includes bibliographical references and index.
Identifiers: LCCN 2016052798 (print) | LCCN 2016054779 (ebook) | ISBN 9781502626097 (library bound) | ISBN 9781502626042 (E-book)
Subjects: LCSH: Bulgaria--Juvenile literature.
Classification: LCC DR55 .S762 2017 (print) | LCC DR55 (ebook) | DDC 949.9--dc23
LC record available at https://lccn.loc.gov/2016052798

Editorial Director: David McNamara
Editor: Kristen Susienka
Copy Editor: Nathan Heidelberger
Associate Art Director: Amy Greenan
Designer: Alan Sliwinski
Production Coordinator: Karol Szymczuk
Photo Research: J8 Media

PICTURE CREDITS

CONTENTS

BULGARIA TODAY

FOR MANY YEARS, BULGARIA WAS A MYSTERY TO THE WORLD. Because of its restrictive Communist government, most people could not travel there, and little was known about what went on inside the country's borders. However, with the fall of Communism in the late 1980s and early 1990s, people have learned that there is much more to Bulgaria than its Communist past. Its cities and towns are a charming mix of ancient and modern, boasting layer upon layer of a rich and exciting heritage.

Bulgaria is a stronghold of Slavic traditions and language, where elements of a deeply rooted folk culture are preserved. It is also a land of mythical beauty, with a long and dramatic history. Its people are resilient and courageous. Over the centuries, they have risen above a succession of repressive empires, including the Roman, Byzantine, and Ottoman. The influence of its multiple cultures can be tasted in Bulgarian cuisine, heard in its music, and seen in its ancient architecture. At the same time, Bulgaria is a part of the modern world. This blend of the oldest and the newest is Bulgaria today.

A woman wearing a traditional folk costume enjoys a festival in Bulgaria.

The physical landscape of Bulgaria is amazingly beautiful. It is a land of great diversity, from fertile, rolling plains to high mountains to the coast of the sea. Many different animals and plants make their home in Bulgaria, including many not found anywhere else. Unfortunately, years of heavy and poorly managed industry, combined with a lack of waste treatment and laws against pollution, have severely damaged much of Bulgaria's environment and put many of the nation's natural resources in danger.

Bulgaria also has a deep and rich history. Its location at the heart of Eastern Europe made it the crossroads for trading routes during ancient times. This easy accessibility led to a number of different ethnic groups and cultures coming to Bulgaria, creating a wave of conquests that led to a diverse population. A major part of the nation's twentieth-century history was dictated by the Communists, who came to power after World War II, when the Soviet Union took control of Eastern Europe. Life was harsh and gray under Communist rule, but the Bulgarian people did not lose their spirit. By 1989, Communist regimes all over Europe were toppling, and Bulgaria began the uncertain but hopeful process of becoming a democracy.

Religion has been a key part of Bulgaria's culture since the earliest days. The country owes its Slavic alphabet to religious missionaries, who made sure the language was kept alive and used in both religious and social rituals. While the Bulgarian Orthodox Church is the most popular religious authority in Bulgaria, the nation is also home to Muslims, Jews, and other Christians, creating a diverse society.

The heart of Bulgaria is its people, who value family life above all and enjoy living in extended families. Grandparents are important members of the family and play a major role in raising children. Special holidays honor grandparents and express the love different generations have for each other. Even though Bulgaria is a modern nation, it still holds fast to its rich folk traditions. This love is expressed through the nation's unique foods, special festivals, iconic artwork, and the everyday pleasures of the Bulgarian population.

Bulgaria has lots of wildlife living in its forests, such as deer.

GEOGRAPHY

Forests and hills give way to the beautiful coastline of the Black Sea.

BULGARIA IS LOCATED IN THE HEART of southeastern Europe. The east coast of the country is bordered by the Black Sea. This sea has been very important to Bulgaria's economy and history for centuries because it provided passage to the Mediterranean Sea, one of the most important bodies of water in Europe. The Black Sea connects to the Mediterranean through the Sea of Marmara.

Bulgaria borders several other countries. Turkey lies to the southeast, while Greece is located along the southwestern border. Macedonia and Serbia border Bulgaria on the west. The Danube River separates Bulgaria from Romania, its neighbor to the north. The total area of Bulgaria is 42,810 square miles (110,879 square kilometers). Bulgaria is not a large country. It is only a bit larger than the state of Tennessee in the United States.

The country is divided into three regions. A range of mountains known as the Balkans divides the country into north and south. The third region is located along the coast of the Black Sea.

Although Bulgaria is a small country, it has an amazing variety of natural landscapes. Bulgaria contains majestic mountains and fertile plains and lowlands. It also features a beautiful coastline. The landscape has so much variety that a surprise waits around every corner.

BULGARIA'S THREE REGIONS

The Balkan Mountains divide the country into two parts. The fertile Danubian Plain covers the north. A region of high mountains, enclosed valleys, and the large Thracian Plain lies in the south. The third distinct area is the Black Sea coast.

Northern Bulgaria has been the country's golden granary since the seventh century, when the Slav and Bulgar tribes united to form the beginning of Bulgaria. In recent times, a prosperous food and beverage industry has developed in the region, based on the production of grains and oilseeds.

Veliko Türnovo, called Turnovo or Türnovo for short, is one of Bulgaria's oldest cities and overlooks the winding Yantra River. Its stone fortress walls testify to its importance as the medieval capital. However, in modern-day Turnovo, heavy industry is very significant, although the city still boasts many historical monuments, such as churches and castles.

In southern Bulgaria, warm Mediterranean air reaches the region along the river valleys, and the Balkan Mountains act as a climatic barrier against

cold northern influences. These weather conditions, along with fertile soils and abundant mountain waters, create favorable conditions to grow vegetables, fruits such as grapes, and cotton. The Bulgarian oil-bearing rose also thrives there.

The Tsarevets Fortress in Veliko Türnovo.

Most of the big cities in southern Bulgaria, including the capital, Sofia, are encircled by prosperous farms. This region is also home to light industry, including tobacco processing and textiles. Heavy industry, such as nonferrous metallurgy, machine making, chemicals manufacturing, timber processing, and cement production, is also found in this area.

The highest mountains in the Balkan Peninsula rise in the southwest of Bulgaria. The rugged profiles of the Rila and Pirin Mountains attract hikers and skiers from all over Europe, while the gently rolling slopes of the Rhodope Mountains provide excellent conditions for winter tourism. Vast mountain pastures enable cattle breeding and sheep raising.

The eastern parts of the Rhodope are inhabited mainly by Bulgarian Turks, who make good use of the favorable soils and the sunny, arid climate to cultivate top-grade tobacco.

YOGURT IN BULGARIA

Yogurt being made here is a staple of the Bulgarian diet. It can be eaten plain or made into a drink, salad dressing, or cold soup. Bulgarian yogurt is usually made from cow's milk, but sheep's or goat's milk are also used. Yogurt from sheep's milk is considered a delicacy.

The bacteria responsible for the fermentation of Bulgarian yogurt thrives best only within the country. Bulgarians believe that, apart from being a rich source of calcium, their yogurt also contributes to their longevity.

A LAND OF CAVES AND BEACHES

The country's eastern coastline is approximately 219 miles (352 kilometers) long. This is the Black Sea coast, where steep cliffs with underwater caves alternate with long sandy beaches, and jungle-like vegetation grows around the mouths of rivers. Small picturesque fishing towns lie side by side with large industrial port cities. Well-developed industries in this region include petrochemical, shipbuilding, metal processing, and electrical appliance industries. Raw materials are imported, and finished products are exported to numerous other countries.

A VARIETY OF SEASONS

Bulgaria has a temperate continental climate. However, the weather is affected by diverse elements, such as the humid cyclones of the North Atlantic, the severe anticyclones of the Siberian plain, and mild air currents that waft in from the Mediterranean Sea.

The average annual temperatures are about 51 degrees Fahrenheit (11 degrees Celsius) for northern Bulgaria and 56°F (13°C) for southern Bulgaria.

The coldest winter month is January, when temperatures average 23°F (−5°C) in the north and up to 36°F (2°C) in the south. It is much colder in the mountains, while winters at the Black Sea coast are milder, with temperatures averaging around 36°F (2°C). Summers are hot but tolerable. July is the hottest month for the whole country, with temperatures hovering between 70 and 75°F (21 and 24°C), although it is cooler in the high mountains.

Rain is the most common precipitation, but there are heavy winter snowfalls across the northern plains and in the mountains. Precipitation is evenly distributed across the country and throughout the four seasons.

Because of the diverse terrain, there are no tornadoes, hurricanes, sandstorms, or other strong winds of that nature. The only constant air currents are the fresh breezes along the seacoast.

A LAND OF RIVERS, LAKES, AND SPRINGS

Bulgaria has over 526 rivers, though the only navigable river is the Danube at 300 miles (483 km) long. Other major rivers include the Iskur, which flows northward from the Rila Mountains and through Sofia before joining

Birds nest along the coast of Srebarna Lake.

Bulgaria is home to about 770 types of medicinal plants, including dandelion, St. John's wort, nettles, valerian, mint, deadly nightshade, and poppies. About 250 are processed for trade with other countries, providing a valuable source of income for Bulgaria.

A Bulgarian woman picks roses from a garden to make perfume and rose oil.

the Danube, and the Maritsa, which flows through southern Bulgaria before defining the border between neighboring Greece and Turkey.

There are about 330 lakes in Bulgaria. The largest are the Black Sea lakes, which are believed to have medicinal qualities. Sreburna Lake near the Danube is the habitat of rare birds, such as the pink pelican and the wild swan. The high-mountain glacial lakes in the Rila and Pirin Mountains are popular attractions.

Many natural mineral springs and baths are found all over the country. Bulgaria has some 500 deposits of mineral waters from over 1,600 sources.

PLANTS AND ANIMALS

Bulgaria is a paradise for botanists and nature lovers. It is home to more than 3,750 vascular plant species and 13,000 animal species. It has over

250 native plants, such as the Rila cowslip and Pirin poppy. The Bulgarian oil-bearing rose is the only descendant of the Persian rose surviving in Europe.

Bulgaria is also home to plants that have survived since ancient geological eras. These plants include the Strandja periwinkle, white and black spruce, sycamore, and the near-extinct edelweiss. Dominant varieties of trees include deciduous oak, elm, and beech, together with coniferous pine, fir, and spruce. Bears, wolves, and red deer live in the woods. Bulgaria supports three national parks, eleven nature parks, and ninety wildlife reserves. Reports in the 1990s designated 389 protected plant species and 473 protected animal species.

CITIES AND TOWNS

Most Bulgarians live either in industrialized cities or in villages with an agricultural economic base. As with most countries, geographical conditions dictate where most people settle. Areas with rich farmland will have more settlers than areas that cannot be farmed, and cities that can support industries are much larger and heavily populated than remote cities with little industrialization. In Bulgaria today, there is little difference between the lifestyle of villagers and that of city dwellers. The largest and most prosperous villages are found in the fertile plains of northern and southern Bulgaria, while mountain villages tend to be smaller and poorer. Cities have also seen a large growth in population as young people migrate to them in search of employment, diversity, and more opportunities. This urbanization became a strong trend during the nineteenth century. The process became even more common during the socialist period, when the country developed an industrial base.

Bulgaria has three major cities. They are Sofia, Plovdiv, and Varna.

SOFIA Bulgaria's bustling capital lies at the foot of Mount Vitosha and has a population of 1.25 million. It was built on the site of an ancient Roman fortress, remains of which can still be seen in the underpasses in the city center. Architecturally, Sofia is a mix of early-twentieth-century Baroque buildings and Byzantine-style churches, with a sprinkling of mosques and

A typical street scene in Sofia, Bulgaria's capital and its largest city.

Turkish baths, massive concrete socialist structures dating from the 1950s, and modern glass buildings popular during the 1990s.

Sofia became the capital in 1879 after Bulgaria gained independence from the Turkish Ottoman Empire. At the time, the young capital was no bigger than a village. Today, however, it is the country's largest city and its political, cultural, and commercial center.

PLOVDIV Founded in 432 BCE, the country's second-largest city lies on both sides of the Maritsa River in the middle of the Thracian Plain. It is one of Europe's oldest cities and has a population of about 342,000. Cobblestone streets twist up the hillsides of the Old Town, crowded with ancient ruins and buildings from the eighteenth and nineteenth centuries, built in typical National Revival style.

VARNA This is Bulgaria's third-largest city, with a population of about 333,000. Along with Burgas, it is one of Bulgaria's most important port cities. Known to the ancient Greeks as Odessus, Varna is now an important industrial, transportation, and cultural center. Several luxury resorts line the beaches adjacent to the city. In the summer, hordes of tourists from all over the world flock to these resorts for a taste of what the "Summer Capital" has to offer.

The Balabanov House Museum in Plovdiv shows the National Revival style of architecture.

INTERNET LINKS

http://bulgariatravel.org/en/dynamic_page/74
This site has many facts about Bulgaria's climate and its location in Europe.

http://countrystudies.us/bulgaria/23.htm
This website offers an overview of Bulgaria's landforms and other geographical facts.

http://www.worldatlas.com/geography/bulgariageography.htm
This site includes brief facts about Bulgaria's geography, as well as several maps.

HISTORY

СВЕТИ
БОРИС I

ЦАР
ПОКРЬСТИТЕЛ

This statue of Boris I stands in Pliska, Bulgaria.

2

THOUSANDS OF YEARS AGO, ancient civiliazations made their marks on what would become Bulgaria. The ancient Thracian, Greek, Roman, and Byzantine civilizations were the first to settle in the Balkan Peninsula, and they all brought elements of their cultures.

The true Bulgarian state, however, did not begin until Slavs started migrating in large numbers to the Balkan Peninsula during the sixth and seventh centuries CE, though the name "Bulgaria" is not Slavic at all. Instead, the country is named after the nomadic tribe of Bulgars that came from the vast treeless steppes north of the Black Sea. The Bulgars were warriors who followed their chief, Khan Asparukh, who led them in seizing Slavic lands in Moesia and Little Scythia on the northeast fringe of Byzantium. The Bulgars were so strong that the mighty Byzantine Empire was forced to recognize the authority of the Bulgars in the lands they had captured. In this way, various tribes added their cultures to the nation that would become Bulgaria.

FIRST BULGARIAN KINGDOM

In the year 681 CE, a treaty was signed in which the Byzantine rulers agreed to pay tribute to the newly founded state of Slavs and Bulgars, which was known as the First Bulgarian Kingdom. This achievement for the seven Slavic tribes was made possible by their vigorous alliance with the Bulgars.

Bulgaria became a Communist state after 1944 and began to echo the Soviet Union in many spheres. But in some areas, such as central control of the arts, it proved less restrictive than the former Soviet Union.

The old Bulgarian alphabet.

Because Bulgaria now controlled major roads linking Eastern Europe and Asia with the interior of the European continent, it became the focal point of strife and confrontation between East and West in medieval Europe. Bulgaria's first decades were marked by a life-and-death struggle for survival against the Byzantine Empire. This great common effort gave the multiethnic tribes a sense of unity. The country became a barrier against nomadic invasions from the northeast. For these reasons, Bulgaria was a major force for political stability in this part of Europe.

BORIS I'S RULE

The civic peace of the country was protected by a severe legal code introduced by Khan Krum (reigned circa 796—814), who is remembered in history as Krum the Terrible. According to his laws, defamation was punishable by death, robbery by breaking the anklebones, and denying alms to a beggar by the seizure of property in the name of the ruler.

The amalgamation of the Slavs and Bulgars was finally accomplished when a successor, Boris I (reigned 852—889), adopted Orthodox Christianity in the ninth century. This memorable event came after long negotiations with the Church of Rome and the Church in Constantinople, and enabled the Bulgarian Church to win a marked degree of independence. Its link with Constantinople's religion and politics also gave the Bulgarians a classical heritage, a religious structure, Byzantine political and legal concepts, and the best-defined national culture in Europe in that time.

The leaders of Bulgaria were well aware that the Christianization of the country could lead to a Byzantine cultural conquest of Bulgaria. To prevent this, Boris I eagerly adopted the Slavic alphabet created by the Greek missionary brothers Cyril and Methodius. Boris also worked out a plan for spreading the church liturgy and learning—not in Greek, but in the spoken Slavic language and the new Cyrillic lettering of his country. The Bulgarian national identity was thus forged through the new state religion, the growth and spread of education, and the development of the Bulgarian language.

The First Bulgarian Kingdom reached the zenith of its political, military, social, and cultural development during the reign of Czar Simeon (reigned 893—927), known as the Bulgarian Charlemagne. He made a determined effort to oust the Byzantine Empire from the Balkan Peninsula and to gain recognition for himself as an emperor in the medieval family of Christian monarchs.

THE RISE OF BULGARIAN CULTURE

Bulgaria's golden age was marked by a surge toward political and religious equality with Byzantium, the territorial expansion of Bulgaria over the greater part of the Balkans, and by a flowering of Bulgarian culture.

The new capital city of Preslav was renowned for its magnificent architecture. Along with Ohrid at the opposite end of Czar Simeon's empire, Preslav emerged as a leading center of Slavic literature and culture.

Bishop Clement of Ohrid and his students encouraged an enlightened approach to cultural development. Writers of the period were intensely conscious of their role as champions of the new Slavic culture. Having incorporated much from Byzantine culture, Bulgaria in turn influenced the Serbs, Russians, and Romanians.

The ruins of the ancient capital of Preslav include the king's castle, along with churches and homes.

BYZANTINE CONQUEST

Czar Simeon had followed his father, Boris I, but after Simeon's death, the Bulgarian kingdom plunged into a deep social and political crisis and eventually fell to Byzantium. The eastern Bulgarian provinces and the capital, Preslav, were captured in 971 CE. The southeastern provinces, with Ohrid as the new state capital, held off defeat for a long time, but were finally conquered in 1018 by the Byzantine emperor Basil II, who was nicknamed the Bulgar Slayer.

For over a century and a half of Byzantine colonization, the Bulgarian people suffered excessive taxation, systematic destruction of their literature and their cultural monuments, and other forms of abuse. Yet throughout those years, they kept alive a spirit of freedom and resistance. Numerous uprisings and rebellions against the Byzantine rulers shook the foundations of the empire. The armed resistance of the Bulgarian feudal lords was backed by the vast Bogomil movement—a religious and social organization whose ideology embodied strongly felt anti-Byzantine trends.

In 1185, the aristocratic bolyar (or boyar) brothers Ivan and Petar Asen led a movement to free Bulgarians in the lands between the Danube River and the Balkan Mountains. This led to the establishment of the Second Bulgarian Kingdom, with the Balkan fortress of Veliko Türnovo as the capital. Kaloyan, who succeeded the Asen brothers, completed the liberation of the Bulgarian population of Thrace, the Rhodope region, and Macedonia. His diplomacy led to the recognition of the kingdom by Byzantium and papal Rome.

The restored kingdom's greatest triumph came during the reign of Ivan Asen II (reigned 1218–1241). His skillful diplomatic maneuvers expanded Bulgaria's territory. Once again it stretched "from sea to shining sea," from the Black Sea to the Adriatic, as it had during Czar Simeon's Golden Age.

A NEW CONSTANTINOPLE

Veliko Türnovo was called the city that was "saved by God," "a second Rome," and "a new Constantinople." The vast Bulgarian state saw a new cultural and economic upsurge. It extended its political and trade relations with a number of European states. There was an enormous surge in the construction of churches, fortresses, and bridges. Aristocratic patronage of trades and the arts flourished as never before.

Despite its success, by the second half of the thirteenth century, Bulgaria faced another grave political crisis. A peasant revolt and fierce attacks from Mongol tribes had weakened the nation, making it easy prey for the new great power that was rising in the east of Europe—the Ottoman Empire.

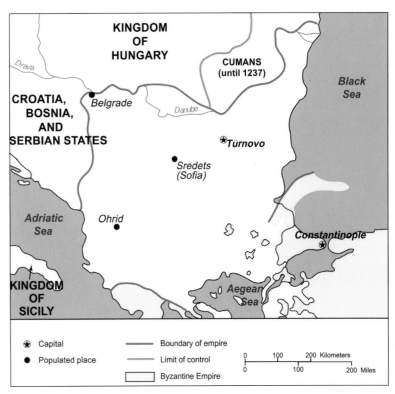

This map shows the Second Bulgarian Empire under Ivan Asen II, who ruled from 1218 to 1241.

CONQUEST AND PERSECUTION

In the last half of the fourteenth century, the Ottoman Empire conquered the Bulgarian people and their divided rulers. This conquest halted the development of the independent Bulgarian state for nearly five centuries. Hundreds of settlements, fortresses, churches, and monasteries were reduced to ashes by the Ottoman invaders. Bulgaria's political and spiritual leaders were exiled or killed, and the clergy was dispersed or ruthlessly repressed. Constantinople took control of the national Bulgarian Church. Bulgarians were excluded from local administration, and all of the country's resources were put at the disposal of the Ottoman war machine.

The conquest was marked by a massive slaughter of soldiers and civilians. Tens of thousands of Bulgarians were sold in the slave markets, while thousands more sought refuge abroad. Christians were forced to convert to Islam or were forced to move to the Asian parts of the Ottoman Empire.

To some extent, this fanatic persecution of the Bulgarian people roused national and religious feelings. The repression compelled them to define their national identity and preserve their cultural traditions and values. They

This fourteenth-century piece shows the intricacy of Ottoman art.

succeeded in doing this against great odds. From the peasants in secluded mountain villages to the monks in the few surviving monasteries, everyone made a contribution. Members of an underground movement called the *haidouks* (hai-DOOKS) also worked to free Bulgaria from Turkish domination.

By the eighteenth century, the spirit of the people was stirred by several factors, including the economic upsurge of the Bulgarian community within the Ottoman Empire, its commercial contacts with people from near and distant lands, and the influence of the European Enlightenment movement that rejected many traditional ideas.

Father Paisiy Hilendarski from the Chilendar Monastery on Mount Athos in Greece was the first to spur the Bulgarian people into action. In 1762, the monk completed his *Slav-Bulgarian History*, an ardent nationalistic appeal to the Bulgarian people to cherish their language and culture, take pride in their glorious historical past, and continue to fight for their liberation from the oppressive Ottomans.

THE RISE OF NATIONALISM

In the first half of the nineteenth century, the momentum for a national revival became even stronger. Schools and library clubs opened in Bulgaria's towns and villages. This movement inspired literature and journalism. Church and urban architecture also flourished, along with the visual arts.

In 1870, the Ottoman government finally gave in to the long and determined struggle of the Bulgarians for a national church separate from the Greek Patriarchate. The independent Church of the Bulgarian Exarchate became the first national political institution to be recognized by Turkey.

The purest figure of the liberation movement was Vassil Levski (1837–1873), called "the Apostle of Freedom" by peasants and scholars alike. Levski was a saint of the revolution. Guided by an unflinching confidence in the Bulgarian national spirit, he decided his country could be liberated only with the participation of the entire population. Levski devoted his boundless energy and organizational talent to underground work in towns and villages throughout Bulgaria.

Apart from setting up local revolutionary committees, Levski drew up the statutes of the organization. Here is how he envisioned the democratic future of his beloved country:

"In our Bulgaria things will be different from how they are in Turkey now. All the nationalities in our country, Turks, Jews, and others, will live under the same pure and sacred laws.

"There will be no king in Bulgaria, but 'popular rule' and to each 'his due.' … A free and pure republic.

"We yearn to see our fatherland free, and when that day comes I will be content just to keep watch over the ducks at pasture."

Betrayed by a fellow Bulgarian and captured by the Turks, Levski was hanged outside Sofia on February 18, 1873. To this day, Bulgarians commemorate his life and death by laying flowers on the modest monument that marks the place of his execution.

A VIOLENT CHANGE

Nationalistic fervor led to an armed revolutionary campaign called the National Revival. This campaign tried to liberate Bulgaria from Ottoman domination. The movement culminated in the April Uprising of 1876, which was suppressed with unprecedented cruelty and vengeance. The Ottoman

army and insurgent bands slaughtered men, women, and children. Some eighty Bulgarian villages were incinerated and their inhabitants massacred.

On their way to the gallows, the organizers of the National Revival revolt rejoiced that their goal had been achieved and expressed their faith in Slavic solidarity. One of them, the military commander Georgi Benkovski, rejoiced, exclaiming, "Such a mortal wound have I inflicted to the heart of the tyrant that he will never recover from it. As for Russia—she is now welcome!"

In 1877, Russia did declare war on the Ottoman Empire, and thousands of Bulgarians volunteered their services. Finally, on March 3, 1878, Turkey signed a treaty of capitulation called the San Stefano peace settlement, recognizing Bulgaria's independence.

ISSUES OVER MACEDONIA

The San Stefano settlement ensured the political liberation of the Bulgarians in Moesia (between the Danube River and the Balkan Mountains), northern Thrace, and Macedonia. Under the sovereignty of its very own church and state, the Bulgarian nation felt free, united, and poised for a great future ahead.

However, the dream was shattered a short five months later by the Berlin Congress of the European superpowers. To satisfy the claims of England and Austria, the Bulgarian state had three of its main provinces snatched away, with only Moesia and the region around Sofia retaining their status. Thrace was renamed Eastern Rumelia and was returned to the Ottoman Empire, along with Macedonia and the Aegean coast. The decisions of the Berlin Congress destroyed hope for national unity and damaged Bulgaria's political, economic, and cultural development for a long time. The decisions also planted the explosive "Macedonian Question" in European politics.

Bulgaria did not resign itself to the slicing up of its nation. The Eastern Rumelia province proclaimed its alliance with the principality of Bulgaria in 1885, and the population of southern Thrace and Macedonia struggled to regain their liberty, but their efforts were unsuccessful.

DARK DAYS OF WAR

Until World War II, Bulgaria pursued the dream of restoring the lands of the San Stefano Treaty and engaged in a series of ill-fated Balkan wars. After repelling a Serbian invasion only weeks after the unification of 1885, the fledgling Bulgarian state formed a new alliance with Greece, Serbia, and Montenegro.

After the First Balkan War in 1912, the alliance forced Turkey to give up its remaining Balkan territories, but extremist nationalistic fervor split up the new alliance. This consequently led to the Second Balkan War in 1913, which was fought by Bulgaria, Romania, Serbia, Greece, and Turkey. This conflict ended in a national catastrophe for Bulgaria, as territory was lost.

World War I tore away even more lands from the country and ruined its industry and agriculture, all of which resulted in a severe political crisis. Crushed and humiliated, Bulgaria completely lost faith in her nationalistic ideals.

THE SOVIETS TAKE CONTROL

During World War II, Bulgaria was a reluctant ally of Germany. It declared a symbolic war on Great Britain and the United States, but its government did

The summer of 1990 was an uneasy time for Bulgarian politicians in power, as ordinary people, students, and the country's intellectuals poured out in thousands demanding better mandates for their nation.

Officers during the First Balkan War in 1912.

not send troops into combat and declined to deport Bulgarian Jews to the death camps of Poland.

In September 1944, while the Bulgarian government was conducting peace talks with the Allies, the Soviet Union declared war on Bulgaria. In conjunction with the Soviet offensive, power in Sofia was seized by a Communist-led coalition called the Fatherland Front.

The stage was thus set for the communization of the country, and the process was completed two years later, despite resistance from democratic forces. Bulgaria then became known as the Soviet Union's most faithful ally, copying the twists and turns of Soviet policies. With the Communist Party in charge, state ownership became the order of the day, and all aspects of the economy fell under state control.

Nevertheless, the Bulgarian model was in some ways significantly different from the Soviet system. For example, Bulgaria's government paid more careful attention to agriculture, raising the rural population's living standards, and the country's achievements in foreign trade were fairly impressive.

A DIFFICULT ROAD TO DEMOCRACY

Bulgaria's "gentle revolution" began with the forced resignation of the dictator Todor Zhivkov in November 1989. Zhivkov's fall set off a wave of rallies. Tens of thousands of demonstrators converged on the central squares of the capital and the big cities, demanding free elections and the end of the regime.

To the credit of those involved, including the reforming wing of the Communist Party, which took over from Zhivkov's old guard, and the young alliance of democratic organizations, Bulgaria managed to break away from Communist rule without bloodshed and violence.

Lengthy negotiations went on between the reforming Communist Party, renamed the Bulgarian Socialist Party (BSP), and the Union of Democratic Forces (UDF). The talks led to an agreement on how elections for a Grand National Assembly were to be held. The assembly's task was to work out a new democratic constitution, and that was accomplished in 1991.

Nazi tanks ride through a village street in Bulgaria in 1941.

After the Soviet Union extended its control over most of Eastern Europe following World War II, Bulgaria and other countries were ruled by Communist governments. Before long, however, public protests and a new generation of rulers pushed all of Eastern Europe to renounce Communism and replace it with more democratic forms of government. The revolutionary movement began in Poland, led by labor unions. By 1989, the movement had spread to East Germany, Hungary, Romania, Czechoslovakia, Bulgaria, and other Eastern Bloc nations. The fall of the Berlin Wall on November 9, 1989, was perhaps the most symbolic and exciting moment of the tremendous change sweeping Eastern Europe.

After the initial political elation over the first taste of freedom, the country was confronted with a far more daunting prospect. The wounds of a nation divided over its Communist past had to be healed, the economy was in tatters and needed mending, and the country had to be made a welcome part of the new unified Europe.

In 1990, Bulgaria had its first taste of democracy when Zheliu Zhelev of the UDF became its first postwar non-Communist president. Zhelev served from 1990 to 1997. The 1990s were marked by constant public unrest, political instability, and economic crises, as the republic embarked on its transition into a free-market economy after the collapse of the Soviet system. In 2001, the abolished Bulgarian monarchy made a dramatic comeback when the former king, Simeon Saxe-Coburg-Gotha, was elected prime minister, a position he retained until 2005. However, rapid inflation, high unemployment, and continued economic uncertainty caused widespread disillusionment in the early 2000s. Under Simeon, the country pressed ahead with reforms and eventually achieved growth. Unemployment fell from the high of 20 percent, inflation came under control, and foreign relations improved. In 2006, progress continued under the stewardship of Bulgaria's new prime minister, Sergei Stanishev, and president, Georgi Parvanov.

Although Bulgaria is on a strong path, it still faces many challenges. Different political groups continue to battle for control, and there is no

In 2004, Bulgaria officially became a member of the North Atlantic Treaty Organization (NATO), and it joined the European Union (EU) in 2007. The prospect of EU membership had, in the years leading to integration into the EU, stimulated a variety of market reforms designed to meet EU economic standards and entry requirements. However, by 2013, Bulgaria was the poorest member of the EU, with a severe lack of jobs for young people. In 2013, the government resigned and was replaced by a socialist ruling party, but corruption and economic problems continued.

dominant force shaping the country's future. Socialism remains strong in the nation, creating a link it to its Communist past that is difficult to overcome, especially in the face of world economic troubles and unrest. Like other European nations, Bulgaria faces a difficult future in a complicated world.

INTERNET LINKS

http://news.bbc.co.uk/2/hi/europe/country_profiles/1061402.stm
This detailed timeline shows important events in Bulgarian history up to 2012.

http://www.bulgaria-embassy.org/History_of_Bulgaria.htm
This website gives a history of the nation from ancient times to the Communist takeover in 1944.

http://www.localhistories.org/bulgaria.html
This site has a great deal of information about Bulgaria's history, from ancient to modern times.

GOVERNMENT

Bulgaria's flag and coat of arms.

3

BULGARIA HAS HAD MANY DIFFERENT types of governments over the centuries, but perhaps none left a stronger mark than the Communist rule during most of the twentieth century. Even after the fall of Communism in 1990, Bulgaria continued to struggle to find a stable form of government.

Today, Bulgaria is a parliamentary democracy in which the prime minister holds the most powerful executive position. Although the constitution once guaranteed the Communist Party the right to absolute political power, today power is in the hands of the people, who exert it directly through freely elected legislative and executive bodies.

JOURNEY TOWARD DEMOCRACY

The democratic process began in 1989 when a group of younger members of the Bulgarian Communist Party failed to see eye to eye with the older, more conservative members of the party. The younger members were influenced by the reforms and political changes in the Soviet Union under President Mikhail Gorbachev and pressed for a more open domestic policy. The dictator, Todor Zhivkov, was forced to resign and was replaced by Petar Mladenov, his foreign minister, who had been leading the drive for reform.

The party changed its name to the Bulgarian Socialist Party (BSP) and commented publicly on the corruption and failings of the old regime.

In the years since the collapse of Communism in 1990, Bulgaria has managed to strengthen its democratic governance system with a stable parliament, reliable government structures, an active civil society, and a free media.

Although the BSP refused to surrender property accumulated by the regime, it was evident that it no longer was a solid dictatorial power. Splinter groups formed, pressing for reform and public accountability. Some of these new groups became independent political parties.

The young opposition began to gather huge support. They held rallies in the streets of Sofia and other big cities. Vast numbers of Bulgarians attended their rallies, demanding that the Communists step down from power.

A NEW CONSTITUTION

After the fall of Communism, the new constitution of the Republic of Bulgaria was ratified on July 12, 1991. After a period of deep instability in the 1990s, governance in Bulgaria was stabilized in 2001 with the election of Simeon Saxe-Coburg-Gotha as prime minister.

For forty-five years, the Bulgarian Communist Party (BCP) had a constitutionally guaranteed right to authority in the country. It commanded all aspects of social, economic, cultural, and educational life. Membership in the party was high compared with ruling Communist parties in other countries. As a political power, it had a long and tumultuous history.

Founded as a workers' social-democratic party in 1891, it was renamed the Bulgarian Communist Party in 1919. Its Communist symbols were even incorporated into the state coat of arms. It became a cofounder and an active member of the Third Communist International. After the seizure of power by the military-royalist coalition in 1923, the leadership of the BCP fled to Moscow. Until World War II, the party led a double life as an underground political force within the country, while its surviving leaders were sheltered abroad.

During World War II, the underground BCP committed acts of sabotage and assassinated police officials and fascist functionaries, but did not organize a general insurrection. The BCP's road to power began with two concurrent events: Soviet troops crossed into Bulgaria in September 1944, and Sofia was seized by the leftist political alliance of the Fatherland Front.

Once in power, the BCP mobilized the army and the economy for the battle against Germany, purged the Fatherland Front coalition of its competitors, and earned Soviet respect as an effective and loyal ally. From this point on, until the emergence of democracy in 1989, the history of the BCP closely followed that of Soviet political life, and its political grip remained firm and virtually uncontested.

EXECUTIVE BRANCH   Bulgaria's president, Rumen Radev (elected in November 2016), is the chief of state and commander of the armed forces. He is largely a symbolic figure, representing national unity. The president and vice president are elected every five years by direct popular vote and can be reelected once. Bulgaria's prime minister is the head of government. The prime minister is selected by the National Assembly (parliament). The prime minister nominates the Council of Ministers (cabinet), which must be

Former prime
minister Boyko
Borisov (*left*) and
former president
Rosen Plevneliev
(*right*) in 2013.

approved by parliament. The council is responsible for managing the state budget, enforcing state policy, and maintaining law and order.

LEGISLATIVE BRANCH The unicameral National Assembly has 240 members, who are elected for four-year terms by direct popular vote. A party must gain at least 4 percent of the popular vote to be represented. The assembly enacts laws, schedules presidential elections, approves prime ministers and cabinet ministers, ratifies international treaties and agreements, and declares war.

JUDICIAL BRANCH The Supreme Administrative Court and the Supreme Court of Cassation (meaning annulling or canceling) are Bulgaria's two highest courts of appeal. The Supreme Judicial Council oversees the system and appoints judges and prosecutors. Its twenty-five members serve five-year terms. The Constitutional Court, consisting of twelve judges serving nine-year terms, interprets the constitutionality of laws and treaties. It can repeal laws that it deems unconstitutional.

ADMINISTRATIVE REGIONS Bulgaria is divided into 28 administrative regions or provinces (*oblasti*), which are subdivided into 265 self-governing municipalities. Sofia and the region surrounding it is a separate jurisdiction, comparable with Washington, DC.

REGIONAL AND LOCAL GOVERNMENT

Regional governors are selected by the Council of Ministers. Municipalities are run by mayors, who serve four-year terms, and by municipal councils, which are directly elected legislative bodies. Local governments enforce policies at the local level, but their revenues depend on the central government.

MANY POLITICAL PARTIES

Three parties that have been prominent in Bulgarian politics since the 1990s are the Bulgarian Socialist Party (BSP, formerly the Bulgarian Communist Party), the Union of Democratic Forces (UDF, a coalition formed in 1989 as opposition to the Communist government), and the Movement for Rights

A woman walks past election posters promoting an ultra-nationalist candidate in 2014.

FREE ELECTIONS

For Bulgarians over the voting age of eighteen, the 1990 parliamentary elections were a most exciting political experience. Yet the elections were also the cause of profound disappointment. Despite massive public demonstrations of unity by the opposition coalition, the anti-Communist votes got dispersed among parties that did not muster the necessary 3 percent of the public vote. The Bulgarian Socialist Party still won the majority of seats in the parliament, but Bulgarians did not resign themselves to continued rule by the BSP.

Shortly after the elections, students at the University of Sofia went on strike, which was a social rebellion without precedent in the history of the nation. The students demanded both an investigation into the fairness of the elections and the resignation of the socialist president, Petar Mladenov, who had called out army tanks in reaction to the widespread demonstrations. The strike built throughout the country, and before long, Mladenov was pressured into resigning. Parliament was in deadlock over the election of a new president since no party could muster the necessary majority.

In the political summer of 1990, a unique movement developed with the aim of forestalling a socialist victory. Led by students and a number of the country's intellectuals, Bulgarians pitched tents in the center of the capital, forming what came to be known as the "City of Truth." Over the next several months, the demonstration grew in size and power, numbering between six thousand to seven thousand people at its height.

and Freedoms (MRF, representing the Turkish minority). A newer party, the Simeon II National Movement (SNM), was founded by former king and prime minister Simeon Saxe-Coburg-Gotha in 2001. For a time, the largest party was Citizens for European Development of Bulgaria (GERB), which was founded in 2006 and was aligned with Prime Minister Boyko Borisov. In November 2016, GERB suffered a defeat in the presidential election to the BSP, and Borisov announced his intention to resign as prime minister.

ELECTIONS BRING CHANGE

Bulgarian citizens eighteen years or older are entitled to vote. Bulgaria's sixth parliamentary election was held on June 25, 2005. The Coalition for Bulgaria, of which BSP is a partner, had a lead with 34.2 percent of votes, but did not have a majority. The ruling party, SNM, was second, with 21.9 percent. Third was MRF, with 13.7 percent. Subsequent parliamentary elections saw the rise of the newly formed GERB party. The presidential election on October 23, 2011, installed GERB candidate Rosen Asenov Plevneliev as president.

Bulgaria faced more changes in the 2016 elections. In May of that year, President Plevneliev indicated that he would not seek a second term as president. Bulgarian elections are not held at one time, but in several stages. In the first stage, most recently held in early November 2016, the winner was Rumen Radev, who has close ties to Russia and wants to end European Union sanctions against Russia. Prime Minister Boyko Borisov had backed a different candidate. When Radev's presidential election was confirmed on November 14, 2016, Borisov announced his intention to resign. These developments caused a great deal of instability in Bulgaria's government as citizens looked ahead to another round of parliamentary elections in 2017.

INTERNET LINKS

http://www.bbc.com/news/world-europe-17202996
This website includes brief profiles of key figures in Bulgaria's government.

http://globaledge.msu.edu/countries/bulgaria/government
This website includes charts and information about Bulgaria's government today.

http://undp.bg/government-bulgaria
Read here for an easy-to-follow guide to how Bulgaria's government works.

ECONOMY

Bulgaria's currency, the lev, features prominent figures and colorful designs.

4

THE COLLAPSE OF COMMUNISM in 1989 had a powerful effect on Bulgaria's economy, just as it did in other nations struggling to adjust to life after Communism. Bulgaria's Communist economy was based on complete control from the state, which owned everything and ran everything. After Bulgaria's socialist economy collapsed, the country was forced to reform its centralized economy into a free-market economy. For the first time, people could own their own businesses and property, and decide how to make money. For many, this was a very difficult transition.

In addition, the socialist system itself left many problems in its wake. Bulgaria started the 1990s with an unwieldy economic structure and a daunting national debt. The country had concentrated too much on heavy industry without building up energy supplies and natural resources. As a result of this imbalance, along with chaotic management, the early and mid-1990s saw a steep drop in agricultural and industrial productivity. Inflation and unemployment rates skyrocketed.

Bulgaria's fishing industry remains important to the country's economy. Two main sources for the industry are the Danube River and the Black Sea.

SHOCKING REFORMS

The new government embarked on a series of economic reforms in 1991, based on monetary "shock therapy." Inflation was curbed by a drastic increase in all prices and interest rates, and by withdrawing state subsidies from ineffective enterprises. While these measures did eventually succeed in stabilizing the annual inflation rate, they badly sidelined the country's economic development and reduced the living standards of the people.

With international support, Bulgaria adopted further reforms in 1997 that included major trade and price liberalization, social sector reforms, establishment of a currency board, and divestiture of state-owned enterprises. This successfully turned around Bulgaria's economy, lowered inflation, and boosted investor confidence. The private sector also grew rapidly, contributing to 64 percent of the country's gross domestic product (GDP) in 2004.

In 2003, the EU declared Bulgaria a fully functioning market economy. In 2005, Bulgaria's GDP growth rate was 5.5 percent. However, the downturn in global markets made it impossible for Bulgaria's economy to grow. In 2014, the nation's GDP growth rate was only 3 percent. The government's recent efforts to improve the economy have focused on reducing taxes, curbing corruption, and increasing foreign investment. Bulgaria's unit of currency is the lev, although it is on the path to switch to the euro.

SOVIET INDUSTRY

Before World War II, industrial enterprises were mostly those of textile production, food processing, and woodworking. There was no heavy industry to speak of, as power sources and technical facilities were rudimentary. After the war, under Soviet influence, the economy was reorganized and tied to the Soviet economic model.

Bulgaria wanted to catch up with the industrialized nations by setting up heavy industry. It concentrated on heavy machinery production and on chemical and metallurgy plants, even though the country lacked both natural resources and export markets. At the same time, the government curtailed

the development of light industries—mainly consumer products—despite the fact that the country had considerable experience and a good international reputation in that area.

Bulgaria paid a high price for these changes. The result was that the country could not afford to keep up with the latest technological developments in heavy industry. Nor could it compete in the international market on price and quality. Its huge plants soon became outdated. To upgrade them, the government had to resort to high-interest loans, which added to the fast-growing national debt.

INDUSTRY TODAY

Today, industry makes up 27.6 percent of the GDP. Since the major economic crisis of 1997, the government has been committed to economic reform and fiscal planning. Bulgaria's industrial sector grew slowly but steadily in the early 2000s. Low inflation and structural reforms improved the business environment and attracted direct foreign investment.

The performance of individual industries has been varied. Food and tobacco processing, together with the electronics industry, suffered from the

Oil refining survived the 1990s because of a strong export market and the takeover of Burgas Refinery by Russian oil giant LUKoil. The chemical industry has also done well but is subject to fluctuating natural gas prices. Mining, however, has declined. Bulgaria is rich in minerals such as copper, gold, iron, lead, and zinc, but many deposits remain unexcavated because of a lack of modern equipment and funding.

The construction industry met with a downturn in the 1990s when industrial and housing projects declined, but made a recovery in the early 2000s. The sector, now dominated by private companies, has resumed the foreign building programs that led to prosperity in the Communist era. Shipbuilding has prospered, too, because of foreign ownership and privatization.

loss of Soviet markets and have not been able to compete in Western Europe. Bulgaria's textiles and clothing exports, on the other hand, have performed well in both domestic and international markets.

CHANGES TO THE FISHING INDUSTRY

Bulgaria's fishing industry remains important to the country's economy. Two main sources for the industry are the Danube River and the Black Sea. In 2000 there was a 45 percent drop in marine catches. Although the fish-farming industry (particularly sturgeon) expanded in the early 2000s, the catch from both sources has decreased sharply in recent years, yielding only a few species of fish for domestic markets in 2004. While certain domestic aquaculture production increased between 2004 and 2013, Bulgaria imports increasing amounts of fish. In 2012, the Law on Fisheries and Aquaculture put a ban on commercial fishing in in-country water basins.

AGRICULTURAL STRENGTHS AND WEAKNESSES

Bulgaria's traditionally strong agricultural sector has been hampered by slow reform of the deposed Communist system. Under Communist rule, Bulgaria's agriculture was heavily centralized, integrated with agriculture-related industries, and state run. The estates of large landowners were seized and nationalized, and smaller landowners and stockbreeders were forced into agricultural cooperatives.

To resolve the crisis and return the land to its previous owners, the Bulgarian parliament voted in a new Law of the Land in 1992. This law created a free market, with the aim of allowing landowners to buy and sell land and to form associations and corporations. Few Bulgarians, however, have been given back their land, and even fewer have found the means to cultivate the land that has been returned.

Bulgaria has fertile soil and a mild climate, but only some 2 percent of its arable land is devoted to permanent field crops such as wheat, corn, and barley. Other crops include sugar beets, sunflowers, tobacco, fruits, and vegetables. Tomatoes, cucumbers, and peppers are the major vegetable

Bulgaria still has many agricultural areas, such as this lavender field near Kazanlak.

A tour guide leads a group through the Roman baths, a popular tourist site in Varna.

exports. Bulgaria is one of the world's major tobacco producers. Livestock includes cattle, sheep, poultry, pigs, and buffalo. The main dairy products are yogurt and white cheese. Today, agriculture makes up just 5.1 percent of the nation's GDP.

THE SERVICE INDUSTRY

The services sector is the largest contributor to the GDP at 67.2 percent. Growth has been concentrated in government services, although the quality and kinds of services vary greatly. The Bulgarian banking system was completely reformed in the 1990s and fully privatized in 2003. The tourism industry has also grown rapidly since the early 2000s. In 2004, over 4 million tourists visited Bulgaria, compared with 2.3 million in 2000. By 2013, the number of tourists had increased to more than 5 million.

MODERN TRANSPORTATION

Bulgaria may have many problems, but its transportation system is a success story that its citizens are proud of. Bulgaria's transportation system is modern and efficient. The nation's location on the international commercial routes that cross the Balkan Peninsula and connect Europe, Asia, and Africa made it important for Bulgaria to develop a reliable transportation system. In addition to its train and road systems, Bulgaria also has fifty-seven airports with paved runways and comprehensive transportation along the Danube River and across the Black Sea.

TRAVEL BY TRAIN Most of the country's railroad system was built before World War II. By 2002, the railways totaled 3,967 miles (6,384 km). Sofia is the hub of both domestic and international rail connections. Large cities are connected by express trains. Freight transportation is also big business; in 2014, 3,439 tons (3,120 metric tons) of freight were moved by train. Most Bulgarians prefer to travel by train as it is cheap and reliable.

ROADS In Bulgaria, there are many roads. International highways pass through Bulgaria, the newest being the Trakia Highway. Opened in 2013, it stretches 579 miles (360 km), from Sofia to the city of Burgas on the Black Sea. It is hoped that by 2020 the country will have as many as seven major highways running through the country.

Railroad enthusiasts enjoy a ride on an old Bulgarian steam train.

PORTS Bulgaria has two main ports on the Black Sea, Burgas and Varna. The Black Sea connects the country with the Mediterranean Sea and the rest of the world, and the Danube River is the gateway to Central Europe. The Danube runs along Bulgaria's border for about 300 miles (483 km).

AIRPORTS AND AIRLINES Bulgaria has three international airports—in Sofia, Varna, and Burgas. Sofia Airport is the oldest and largest, and has the busiest air traffic. The national airline company is Bulgaria Air, which flies to most major European cities.

INTERNET LINKS

http://www.focus-economics.com/countries/bulgaria
This site includes an overview and detailed data about Bulgaria's economy today.

http://www.heritage.org/index/country/bulgaria
This site features a very detailed look at where Bulgaria stands today in terms of economic strength and growth.

http://www.worldbank.org/en/country/bulgaria/overview
Here is a concise list of facts accompanied by graphs describing Bulgaria's economic outlook.

ENVIRONMENT

This Bulgarian forest shows the damage from air pollution.

• • • • • • • • • • • • •

A lack of
environmental
planning and
control under past
Communist rule
has taken a toll on
Bulgaria's cities.

5

HEAVY INDUSTRIES—LIKE TRACTOR-making companies and other large machinery companies—might be good for the economy, but they can be a disaster for the environment. This is especially true when governments don't consider the environment and allow factories and other industries to operate however they like. Sadly, this was true in Bulgaria, as well as other Communist countries.

When Bulgaria's heavy industries were set up in the Communist era, nobody considered the threat they might one day pose to the environment. However, it did not take long for people to realize their country's natural environment was in serious trouble in all areas. The problems were many. Heavy industry had caused polluted air in Bulgaria's cities; rivers full of raw sewage, heavy metals, and detergents; forests scarred by acid rain, which resulted from air pollution; and once-fertile soils contaminated with heavy metals from metallurgical plants and other industrial wastes.

The ecological balance was also badly disturbed. Over 40 percent of Bulgaria's population lived in areas with dangerous levels of pollution. The situation was especially dangerous in Devnya, Plovdiv, Varna, Elisseina, Kurdzhali, and Pirdop, where sulfuric oxide emissions were more than three times the permissible limit. Local residents saw a serious rise in respiratory and other pollution-related diseases, with children being the most affected.

PROGRESS AND DANGER

Like other Soviet countries, Bulgaria saw unrestrained industrial development as the pathway to national advancement and progress toward the socialist ideal. The extent of damage done to the environment was not addressed until the government of Todor Zhivkov (1962—1989) was overthrown in 1989.

The Zhivkov government's commitment to its industrial policy and the lack of funds for protective measures forced it to conceal major environmental hazards. Plants and factories that failed to meet environmental standards paid only token fines, and the government had no real incentive to institute changes.

Although environmental awareness has improved in present-day Bulgaria, the state's lack of administrative strength and fears of unemployment have prevented it from clamping down on many dangerous practices.

DAMAGE FROM THE SKIES

None of Bulgaria's major cities has escaped intense air pollution, with Sofia being the worst, as ever-increasing numbers of cars contribute to the smog. The problem stems from the combined emissions of industry, transportation, and energy production.

In the mid-1990s, Bulgaria was among the fifty countries with the highest industrial emissions of carbon dioxide. Airborne pollutants, causing defoliation of natural forest cover, have damaged an estimated 25 percent of Bulgaria's forests.

TRANSPORTATION POISONS Some 70 to 80 percent of Sofia's air pollution is caused by vehicular emissions. In the 1990s, a rapid increase in motor vehicles using leaded fuel exacerbated the problem. Transportation generated 45 percent of total nitrogen oxide emissions, 39.5 percent of carbon emissions, and 13.4 percent of carbon dioxide emissions.

In the early 2000s, however, Sofia began to phase out the use of leaded fuel following the Environment for Europe (EFE) Conference initiatives. Besides promoting the use of unleaded gasoline throughout the region, the Sofia Initiatives established during the conference also aimed at significantly reducing sulfur and particulate emissions.

The sunrise in Sofia is marred by thick clouds of smog from air pollution.

TOXIC ENERGY A major source of toxic emissions comes from thermoelectric power stations. Low-quality brown lignite coal remains an important resource for energy and heat production in Bulgaria. Because of its high sulfur and ash content, lignite is responsible for a high percentage of the total emissions of sulfuric oxides.

Burning coal for electricity releases sulfur dioxide and nitrogen oxide into the air, causing acid rain. Forests, trees, lakes, animals, and plants all suffer from the effects of acid rain. Acid rain can make trees suffer loss of leaves, bark damage, and stunted growth. Fish in the lakes and rivers polluted by acid rain are poisoned, and birds can die from eating the toxic fish. Human health is also affected when people eat fish and other contaminated animals.

In comparison with European standards, Bulgarian industrial technology is characterized by exceptionally low energy efficiency. To make matters worse, there is a high proportion of energy-intensive industries, causing Bulgaria to use many times more energy than average European countries in order to produce every dollar of its GDP.

HIGH RISK FROM INDUSTRY   Bulgaria has many chemical, cement, textile, petrochemical, leather, and oil refining industries, as well as metallurgical plants and factories that produce construction materials. These factories emit high levels of pollutants.

The unsustainable practices of many such heavy industries have created fourteen "hot spots," or high-risk areas affecting local health. These are densely populated towns and villages, where more than one-third of the population resides.

The most heavily polluted hot spot is the region of Maritsa Iztok, where 73 percent of the country's total sulfur oxides, 30 percent of the nitrogen oxides, and 65 percent of the methane are emitted. In 2013, Bulgaria had the worst air pollution in the European Union.

WHERE TO PUT THE WASTE

Waste generation is inevitably linked to economic and social development. The increase in production, consumption, and per-capita income is connected with an increased demand for natural resources and the generation of more pollutants and waste.

Solid waste concentrations in Bulgaria are traditionally very high, and the proportion of recycled waste is small. Traditionally, the most common method for discarding industrial, household, and agricultural waste was to dump it at unregulated landfills. One of the reasons for this was the lack of modern facilities and technology for the processing and disposal of waste, including hazardous materials. With the help of the EU, efforts are under way to correct this problem, though much progress still needs to be made.

SOIL CONTAMINATION   Severe soil contamination and erosion are the result of poor waste-management practices. Industrial pollutants— especially from metallurgic plants and unregulated mines—are responsible for damage to 115 square miles (298 sq km) of land. Toxic waste compounds from copper pyrite and lead-zinc ore processing have also degraded large areas of land. In some areas, the soil is so badly damaged that it cannot be used for agriculture.

WATER SUPPLY WOES

Shortages of drinking water are sometimes experienced by the residents of several regions of Bulgaria. Water losses in the distribution system (up to 60 percent) and high consumption rates by industry (31 percent), together with normal household use, are the main causes of the lack of drinking water.

A European Environment Agency report found that Sofians each used 118 gallons (447 liters) of water per day, compared with only 37 gallons (140 L) used in Brussels, Belgium. Even though widely known, many water-saving measures are not practiced in Bulgarian households.

The Yantra River is the most polluted river in Europe.

Another problem is that natural water resources are unevenly distributed in the territory. There are some areas with low water reserves that are next to areas with relatively abundant supplies. In the past, some villages had no water supply at all. However, in recent years, Bulgaria has improved its water distribution to provide water to all of its citizens.

THE DIRTIEST RIVER IN EUROPE

By the early 1990s, two-thirds of Bulgaria's rivers were already heavily polluted, and the Yantra River was classified as the dirtiest river in Europe. Today, almost all the major rivers and the Black Sea are fouled by factories that dump detergents, heavy metals, nitrates, oils, and untreated sewage

Bulgaria's unique natural resources are subject to many assaults, including the illegal felling of forests for timber and the destruction of natural habitats. The loss and degradation of both aquatic and terrestrial habitats is the biggest threat, affecting all kinds of ecosystems, ranging from the alpine forests to the coastal wetlands.

Pollution of Bulgaria's fertile soils, air, and water has intensified in recent decades and is devastating to both biological diversity and human health. Virtually all forms of industrial, agricultural, transportation, and household pollution are present in the Bulgarian landscape and threaten biological diversity in varying degrees.

The overexploitation of many economically valuable species has affected various ecosystems and habitats. This includes the illegal gathering and export of fungi, medicinal plants, reptiles, and amphibians; excessive fishing and trawling along the Black Sea coast and open waters; and poaching and sport hunting of mammals and birds (especially waterfowl and birds of prey).

directly into the water. The pollution is so severe that the water from the Danube, Iskur, and Maritsa Rivers is not even fit for irrigation.

In 2000, only 25 to 33 percent of industrial wastewater was treated, and the country's municipal wastewater treatment plants served only 36 percent of households and 12 percent of towns. Despite the fact that two of the country's largest industrial cities, Varna and Burgas, are located on the Black Sea coast, wastewater treatment facilities remain inadequate or nonexistent. For many companies, it is cheaper to pollute than to invest in treatment technologies.

In addition, while 95 percent of towns have access to a sewer system, only 3.2 percent of villages have this access. This lack of sewage treatment means that untreated wastewater is dumped into Bulgaria's waterways, causing more pollution.

A LAND OF BIODIVERSITY

Bulgaria covers a mere 1 percent of Europe's area but has greater biodiversity than Germany, Poland, or Great Britain. This is due to its extraordinarily

varied climate, and its geological and topographic conditions. Bulgaria's natural environment is home to 383 bird species (77 percent of those found in Europe), 207 Black Sea and freshwater fish species, 94 mammal species, 36 reptile species, 16 amphibian species, 27,000 insects and other invertebrates, 200 types of edible fungi, and 3,500 to 3,750 vascular plant species.

The nation supports a great number of ecosystems and representative communities that are highly valuable both commercially and ecologically. These include Bulgaria's forests, which cover about 9.6 million acres (3.9 million hectares), or one-third of the territory of the country.

The government's National Biodiversity Conservation Plan is aimed at conserving, strengthening, and restoring key ecosystems, biological species and their genetic resources, and, very important, at ensuring the sustainable use of natural resources. Species conservation is regulated by the Hunting Act (2000), the Medicinal Plants Act (2000), the Fisheries and Aquacultures Act (2001), and, above all, the Biodiversity Act (2002).

Bulgaria's native animals include the white stork and the harbor porpoise,

PROTECTING THE LAND

One of the most important ways of preserving biological diversity is the protection of ecosystems and habitats. Protected areas in Bulgaria cover over 1.2 million acres (485,640 ha), or 4.4 percent of the country, and are regulated by the Protected Areas Act (1998).

A beautiful view of Pirin National Park, a UNESCO World Heritage site.

These areas include 3 national parks, 11 nature parks, 12 people's parks, 475 natural monuments, 125 protected localities, and 90 reserves (including 17 biosphere reserves). The coastal zone is also protected in 12 areas that encompass some 65 percent of the Black Sea coastline.

Bulgaria's three national parks—Pirin, Rila, and Central Balkan—safeguard mountain ecosystems that contain some of the country's most important watersheds and natural resources. The reserves cover a total area of 199,070 acres (80,564 ha) and support forest ecosystems and habitats of rare species, including 60 percent of Bulgaria's total forested area. Today the United Nations recognizes 86 percent of Bulgaria's protected areas and has listed two—the Srebarna Nature Reserve and Pirin National Park—as UNESCO World Heritage sites.

Other high-priority regions for new protected areas or expansion of existing ones are the Rhodope, Strandja, Western Balkan, and Belasica mountain regions; the entire Black Sea coast; areas surrounding and connecting the existing national parks in the Rila, Pirin, Vitosha, and Stara Planina Mountains; and the valleys of the Struma and Danube Rivers.

SAVING ENDANGERED PLANTS AND ANIMALS

Pollution and human activity have caused a number of Bulgarian species to become vulnerable or endangered. The danger covers all living things, from plants to insects, reptiles to mammals, birds to fish. In total, Bulgaria has 473 protected animal species and 389 protected plant species. Some of the most threatened mammals include the Black Sea morik seal, bottlenose dolphin, brown bear, harbor porpoise, and European marbled polecat. Endangered birds include the Dalmatian pelican, ferruginous duck, pigmy cormorant, and red-breasted goose. While Bulgaria has taken steps to protect its endangered species, it has not done enough to prevent continued threats to wildlife all over the nation.

INTERNET LINKS

http://www.eea.europa.eu/soer-2015/countries/bulgaria
This comprehensive report studies the many types of pollution threatening Bulgaria's well-being at the current time.

http://www.nytimes.com/2013/10/15/business/international/bulgarias-air-is-dirtiest-in-europe-study-finds-followed-by-poland.html
This article describes the consequences of Communist industrial growth and air pollution on Bulgaria's environmental health.

http://www.slideshare.net/MaryanneKolarska/endangered-species-in-bulgaria
This slideshow profiles some of the many endangered species in Bulgaria.

BULGARIANS

Bulgarians walk down a city street in Plovdiv.

6

SAY THE WORD "BULGARIAN," AND a number of different ethnic groups come to mind. The nation is made up of several distinct cultures, each with its traditions and history. Ethnic Bulgarians make up 76.9 percent of the population. Turks are the largest minority, accounting for 8 percent. Next come the Roma at 4.4 percent. Less than 1 percent are Pomaks (Muslim Bulgarians), Armenians, Russians, Tatars, Greeks, Circassians, and Gagauz. The rest of the population is of unknown or mixed origin.

Bulgaria's multicultural and multiethnic society is very much linked to its historical and cultural roots. Today's Bulgarians trace their roots back to the ancient Thracians, Illyrians, Bulgars, and Slavs. The Roman, Byzantine, and Ottoman conquerors of the Bulgarian lands also left their mark on the ethnic and cultural makeup of the nation.

Each ethnic group has its own customs and dialects. Some of these date back more than fifteen centuries and originated from the tribes who lived in the Balkans at that time.

ALTRUISM: Do a good deed and cast it into the sea.

DETERMINATION: The dogs are barking, but the caravan moves on.

FATALISM: If evil does not come, worse may arrive.

FEMALE: A woman is an iron shirt.

FRIENDS: For a lean year, a relative; for a misfortune, a friend.

INFALLIBILITY: God is not sinless—He created the world.

NECESSITY: When there's no work to be found, join the army.

RESERVE: As with the czar, so with fire—go neither too close nor too far.

RESPONSIBILITY: Where there are many shepherds, many sheep are lost.

SELF-IMPORTANCE: An empty bag weighs more than a full one.

SELF-INTEREST: The dog barks to guard itself—not the village.

WORK: Work left for later is finished by the devil.

CREATING THE BULGARIAN PEOPLE

Thracians were the earliest inhabitants of the Bulgarian lands, living as far back as the second millennium BCE. Then came the Romans. Both civilizations left their marks on the land and its people. To this day, there are Roman roads, baths, and theaters in the country.

The Slavs came to the Balkan Peninsula in the sixth and seventh centuries CE. They were good farmers and stockbreeders. This large ethnic group gradually assimilated with the Bulgars and the Thracians. The Bulgars, who arrived in the late seventh century, were nomads from the steppes along the Volga River. Of Turanian origin, they allied themselves with the Slavs against the Byzantine Empire, laying the foundations of the Bulgarian state and nation.

PRESERVING CULTURE

In the long periods of Byzantine and Ottoman rule, the Bulgarian people effectively resisted attempts at assimilation. They succeeded in preserving their language, culture, belief system, and lifestyle. Today's Bulgarian culture bears some Turkish and Greek traces but has largely kept its distinct character.

Bulgarians have shown themselves to be fairly tolerant in ethnic and religious matters, in spite of their country's connection to many tribes and peoples throughout its turbulent history. Minority groups generally live in peace and accept each other's differences. Bulgaria is one of the few countries from the former Eastern Bloc where the collapse of Communism did not trigger ethnic bloodshed.

TURKS IN BULGARIA

The Turks are descendants of the Ottomans. They are Sunni Muslim by belief and speak the Turkish language. Most of them live in tight-knit communities in the northeastern and south-central parts of the country. Agriculture is the traditional occupation of the Bulgarian Turks, especially the cultivation of tobacco. The social attitudes and customs of Bulgarian Turks who live in rural areas are highly traditional.

A Bulgarian Turk hangs tobacco leaves to dry.

The Pomaks are a small group of Bulgarian-speaking Muslims who live in the Rhodope Mountains. They are descendants of Bulgarians who had changed their faith from Christianity to Islam, either voluntarily or by force, during Ottoman rule. There is a rather unusual reason behind their conversion. The Rhodope Mountains were favorite hunting grounds for the Turkish sultan, and Pomaks were often called upon to serve the royal hunting parties. But Muslim tradition stipulated that only believers in Islam might serve the sultan, so there followed a sustained effort to change the faith of these mountain people to Islam.

In one of its cultural campaigns of the early 1970s, the Communist government forced the Pomaks to change their Turkish-Arabic names to Slavic equivalents and banned the use of the term "Pomak." Fortunately, no government decree could abolish the cultural traditions of these hardy people. Most Pomaks today still live in isolated mountain villages and have preserved their folk songs, customs, and their old handicrafts of wool weaving and rug making.

AREA OF TENSION Relations between Bulgarians and Turks became particularly strained in the 1980s. Bulgarian political commentators went so far as to argue that eventual Turkish separatism would give Turkey an excuse to intervene and turn Bulgaria into another Cyprus. Others pointed to the high birthrates of the Turks, raising the fear that Bulgarians would become a minority in their own country.

During the nationalistic campaign of the Zhivkov government, the Turks were given the difficult alternative either of surrendering their cultural identity or of leaving the land they had inhabited for centuries. But in recent years, both sides have shown a high degree of diplomacy in dealing with these tensions. Today, the ethnic Turkish party, the Movement for Rights and Freedoms, is a recognized parliamentary power with a decisive voice in the legislative and political life of the country.

THE PLIGHT OF THE ROMA

Numbering about 325,000, the Roma form the third-largest ethnic group in Bulgaria, yet they have little stake in the nation. They speak their own language, Roma, although it has absorbed many Bulgarian words.

The Roma used to live in caravans (horse-drawn covered carts, or trailers) and roam the countryside. A small number of them still travel in the old-style caravans, and a few keep performing bears even now, hoping to collect a few coins during their stops in towns. Today most Roma live in slums on the outskirts of the big cities. They face significantly higher illiteracy and unemployment rates than the rest of the Bulgarian population. Their life expectancy is much shorter than the average Bulgarian's. The Roma are sometimes referred to as Gypsies, though many consider this term to be offensive.

Bulgaria's governments, similar to most governments with a big Roma population, have all failed to deal with the plight of the Roma, who remain at the very bottom of Bulgarian society. Facing abject poverty, chronic unemployment, oppression, discrimination, and exclusion from mainstream society and its expectations, out of desperation many have adopted a life of crime or have chosen to emigrate.

A Roma girl stands in front of her house. The Roma are the poorest group of people in Bulgaria.

MANY MINORITIES

Apart from the Roma and the Pomaks, two other minority groups stand out. The Armenians came to Bulgaria in the early twentieth century, driven from their native land in the Caucasus Mountains after mass slaughters by the Turks. They are city dwellers, speak their own unique language, and adhere to their own Armenian Gregorian Church. Traditionally, the Armenians do exquisite craftwork.

Bulgarian Greeks live mostly in the cities along the Black Sea coast and in the bigger cities in south Bulgaria. They are descendants of old Greek colonists. Although some still speak Greek within the family, their culture and lifestyle differ very little from the Bulgarians.

CHANGING POPULATIONS

Since the beginning of the twentieth century, Bulgarians were discouraged from having many children. This was because of the inheritance practice of peasants with small landholdings, whereby all offspring were given a share of the farm. This led to small parcels of land and large family squabbles.

As a result, low birthrate was the worrisome trend by the time of World War II. Women having to work outside the home also contributed to a low birthrate. Even government programs of the 1960s and 1980s, offering family allowances and maternity leave arrangements, failed to raise the birthrate.

The population had also become increasingly urbanized after 1945 because of the Communist government's industrialization program. Today, almost 74 percent of the population is urban.

In 1991, Bulgaria's population had reached nearly 9 million. In 2006 it was only 7,385,367. The decrease was largely because of intensive emigration after the end of the Communist regime. The population continues to decrease, hitting 7,144,653 in 2016.

The size, age, distribution, and ethnic makeup of Bulgaria's population have all been affected by its migration patterns. During the Balkan Wars in the early twentieth century, genocide in neighboring Turkey, Greece, and Serbia sent huge waves of refugees into Bulgaria.

Few people are aware that the Bulgarian people saved the lives of forty-eight thousand Jews during World War II. Bulgaria was then an ally of Nazi Germany and received territorial favors at the expense of Romania, Yugoslavia, and Greece, but it did not go along with the Nazi goal of eliminating Jews.

Under German pressure, the government of the day introduced some half-hearted anti-Semitic measures. The Bulgarian population, however, responded with sympathy and support for the Jews. Once, when the Jews of Sofia were to be expelled to the rural death camps, the citizens of the capital stopped the Nazis by preventing the Jews from reaching the railway station, and the Jews were sent home. Subsequently, many citizens demonstrated in front of the king's palace, protesting the official anti-Semitism.

In 1943, the Nazis finally exacted an agreement from the Bulgarian commissar for Jewish affairs to deport six thousand "leading Jews" to the Treblinka death camp in Poland. But key intellectuals raised a huge outcry in the media against the plan. Church officials and ordinary farmers from north Bulgaria threatened to lie down on the railway tracks to stop the deportation trains. None of those Jews ever left the country.

The chief rabbi of Sofia was hidden by Bishop Stephan of Sofia, a senior church official, who declared publicly that "God had determined the Jewish fate, and men had no right to torture Jews, and to persecute them."

Faced with such determined and widespread opposition, the government revoked the order, and Jews already taken into custody were released. March 10, the day the death trains were supposed to roll out, came to be known in Bulgaria as the "miracle of the Jewish people."

Migration went the other way, too. Some Bulgarian Greeks left to settle in Greece between 1924 and 1926. In the 1940s, many Bulgarian Jews and Armenians moved to Israel and the Armenian Republic. Over 130,000 Bulgarian Turks migrated to Turkey between 1968 and 1978.

Two large waves of emigration caused Bulgaria's population to fall even further in the 1980s and 1990s. Among those who departed were three hundred thousand Bulgarian Turks from 1985 to 1989, the result of an infamous campaign by the Communist government. The Turks were forced

A Bulgarian woman picks strawberries on a farm in Spain. Many young Bulgarians have left the country in search of jobs in other parts of Europe.

to change their names to Slavic ones, prohibited from speaking Turkish in public, and even banned from circumcising their sons, which is a ritual required by Islam. Those who protested were forced to leave the country.

Migration both into and out of Bulgaria in the twenty-first century continues to rise significantly, especially after Bulgaria became part of the European Union on January 1, 2007. Many Bulgarians leave because they fear that their living costs will soar as the country strives for a European standard of living.

LEAVING FOR THE WEST

Throughout the 1990s and 2000s, many of Bulgaria's skilled and professional people left the country. Bulgaria's transition to a market economy and democracy was accompanied by dramatic changes in social welfare, health care, and the cultural sector.

Frustrated by the deteriorating living standards and the hostile conditions for creative work and research, more than seven hundred thousand Bulgarians moved to countries such as Austria, Canada, France, Germany, and the United States. Most of these hopeful migrants were young and well educated.

STRUGGLES FOR EQUALITY

Presently there are two main classes in Bulgarian society—the wealthy and the impoverished. The country needs an established middle class to secure its economic future and political stability. This balancing class, however, has not yet emerged. In fact, the gap between the very rich and the very poor is constantly widening. None of the governments have succeeded in implementing economic strategies to form a strong middle class. This inequality has led to social dissatisfaction, limited consumer spending, a decrease in the quality of the labor force, an increase in income disparity, and a decline of quality education and health care.

A group of folk dancers pose in front of the Bulgarian flag before a performance.

A WELL-DRESSED PEOPLE

Bulgarian folk costumes are richly ornamented with bright, bold colors. Women's costumes include the *bruchnik* (double apron), the *soukman* (closed tunic), and the *saya* (open tunic). Men's costumes are called the *belodresnik*, which means "white dress," and the *chernodresnik*, literally meaning "black dress," but in practice this is more often brown or blue. Present at village celebrations, festivals, or on special occasions, these costumes vary widely from region to region, and their beloved designs are several centuries old.

Although traditional costumes are worn for festivals and holidays, Bulgarians wear the usual Western clothes for everyday life at work, school, or play. They prefer natural fabrics, such as cotton, wool, and silk, and love to dress up for a night out or a party.

Careful attention to one's clothing is a long-standing Bulgarian tradition. According to an old saying, "The greeting will measure how well you are dressed, the farewell will match how clever you have been."

INTERNET LINKS

http://bulgariatravel.org/en/dynamic_page/78
Visit this website to learn more about Bulgaria's lifestyle and traditions.

http://countrystudies.us/bulgaria/25.htm
This site gives a detailed description of the various ethnic groups in Bulgaria.

LIFESTYLE

Sofia's skyline, surrounded by trees and mountains.

7

EVEN THOUGH BULGARIA WAS ruled by a Communist government that emphasized the state over everything, the nation's belief in family and friends never faded. In fact, years of turmoil, violence, and change have taught Bulgarians just how important family and friends really are. Experience has taught them that close relatives can always be depended on in hard times and can be a valuable source of comfort and care for the young, the old, and the sick.

Bulgarians believe in hard work and perseverance, but they also know how to party and enjoy themselves.

In public places, Bulgarians do not appear to be very welcoming, but once inside a Bulgarian home, the true nature of the Bulgarian people becomes obvious. It would be unheard of for a caller not to be offered a drink or a bite to eat, whether it is a friend who has dropped in casually, the person who delivers the mail, or a complete stranger.

Bulgarians generally do not like the idea of letting the state take care of their loved ones in times of sickness or crisis. If possible, they prefer not to depend on hospitals, nursing homes, or banks. Bulgarians may never think of sending Christmas or birthday cards, but in hard times they will offer their help even before it is asked for. In turn, they will expect the same from others.

CHANGING MARRIAGE TRENDS

For many years, Bulgarians had a conservative outlook about family life. They did not approve of those choosing to remain single, and they frowned upon couples living together without getting married. A gay or lesbian partnership was totally incomprehensible to most Bulgarians. However, things have changed over the past few years. Today, Bulgaria has the lowest marriage rate of any country in the European Union at just 2.9 marriages per 1,000 people. There has also been an increase in the number of children born outside of marriage, which is currently 56 percent in Bulgaria. Also, gay and lesbian partnerships are legal, but people in these relationships do not have the same legal protections as heterosexual couples.

EXTENDED FAMILIES

Many Bulgarian homes have three or even four generations living together. Such a family often includes grandparents, aunts, uncles, and cousins, too. This is partly due to the acute shortage of housing in the cities. Also, because both men and women usually hold full-time jobs, grandparents and other

A young man and his bride pose with members of their families after the wedding.

January 21 is Grandmother's Day, one of the most touching and heartwarming Bulgarian holidays. It is also the professional holiday of obstetricians and gynecologists. In the past, the oldest and most experienced woman in the family would help with the birth of her grandchildren. Women today very rarely give birth at home, but a grandmother's role in bringing up children is still very important and appreciated.

On Grandmother's Day, Bulgarian women visit their grandmother to ceremonially wash her and to present her with a fluffy new towel. The same ritual is enacted in the maternity wards of hospitals, where nurses are given a towel as an acknowledgment of the nurses' part in taking care of the mothers and their newborns.

relatives are available to care for the family's children. This extended-family living arrangement has been common in Bulgaria for centuries.

The different generations living under one roof usually get on well together. When two generations share a home, their roles are clearly defined. The younger people usually earn the living, and the older ones tend the home and help raise the children.

Even when parents live away from their adult children, they often act as foster parents for their grandchildren during the summer months. First cousins, who frequently spend vacations together at their grandparents', may grow as close as brothers and sisters. Children often feel closer to their grandparents than to their parents.

The dream home of every Bulgarian is a multistoried house where parents and their adult children's families can each have their own floor and "will not have to change shoes" to visit each other.

MARRIAGE AND LIVING ARRANGEMENTS

Bulgarians tend to marry for love, although some groups, such as the Roma and Pomaks, still have arranged marriages. Couples often get married when they are young and before their careers are established, so they have little choice but to live with their parents. The high cost of housing also means they are seldom able to move out of the parental home. Children are usually brought up by the extended family.

Except for the Muslim and Roma minorities, most young couples have no more than two children. Stringent family planning is due both to tradition and to economic hardship. Both partners in marriage often preserve a significant degree of emotional and professional independence.

WEDDINGS AND DIVORCES Weddings traditionally take place in early spring or the fall. Preparations start months ahead, usually with the betrothal, or engagement. In the city, betrothal typically takes place at a private party given by the immediate families of the couple. Presents are given, and the couple exchanges rings. Wedding bands are usually placed on the left hand until the wedding, when they are shifted to the right hand. In small villages there may be a large feast to which the whole village is invited. The engagement period is also the time to settle issues of property and money. Weddings are elaborate affairs that start at dawn and often continue overnight.

When a marriage fails to work, the partners are free to divorce. The court procedure, however, is long, expensive, and complicated to allow the partners numerous opportunities to reconsider their decision. Nevertheless, divorce rates are rising, especially in urban communities. About 21 percent of Bulgarian marriages end in divorce.

The children of divorced parents normally live with their mother until they come of age, when they can choose with which parent they wish to live. The father is usually given the right to spend weekends plus several weeks during vacations with his children. He is also required to pay some money for their support.

EQUALITY FOR MEN AND WOMEN

Because men were so often away from home during wars and other periods of unrest, women had to act as managers and providers. This history means that today, Bulgarian women enjoy considerable freedom and equality with men.

Socialism and Communism also treated men and women as equals. During the Communist era, the quality of women's education improved and laws were enacted to create gender equality. Also, because families needed two breadwinners, women had little choice but to go out and work. Bulgarian women make up half the workforce and have excelled in their jobs. Today, women hold jobs in all parts of Bulgarian society and have proved to be talented politicians, professors, legislators, and administrators. Since 1989, Bulgaria has had its first woman vice president, Margarita Popova, and prime minister, Reneta Indzhova.

Bulgarian workers assemble electronics in a factory.

CHILDREN: THE CENTER OF THE FAMILY

Children are probably the most important members of Bulgarian society. Bulgarian parents will sacrifice anything for the well-being and the future of their children. A child's achievement is a far greater source of family pride than material benefits or professional advancement.

Unless children happen to live with healthy and energetic grandparents, they learn to take care of themselves early. By the time they are in their early teens, children commonly prepare meals and set the table for younger children and grandparents. Bulgarian parents expect good behavior and have a low tolerance for waywardness or misbehavior.

Most Bulgarian children remain dependent on their parents right into adulthood. But sooner or later, the roles are reversed, and the younger adults start to look after their aging parents. In this way, parents and children remain dependent on each other throughout their lives.

LIVING AT HOME

It is considered a disgrace if a young adult leaves the parental home before marriage. Unless a promising career is at stake, the parents will be accused of having driven their child away.

Even after marriage, it is common for young couples to live with either set of parents. The young couple might help with utilities and other bills, but most Bulgarians would not dream of asking their children to pay rent. The parents would also contribute toward eventual new homes for their children and help with furnishings and decorations.

STRANGER OR FRIEND?

Bulgarians do not reach out to strangers. Even in a small village, strangers get only a hesitant "hello." In the cities, people tend to ignore each other, for the most part.

On the other hand, Bulgarians are kind and generous to anyone who enters their homes. There is a moving Christmas tradition that clearly shows Bulgarian hospitality. The woman of the house brings out a Christmas pie stuck with little dogwood twigs that are to tell each family member their luck for the coming year. But before she serves the pie, the hostess sets aside a piece for "Grandpa Vassil"—the stranger who has not managed to make it home through the snow-covered country roads.

A family has set aside a slice of traditional Christmas pie for Grandpa Vassil, an old Bulgarian tradition.

LIFE IN CITIES AND TOWNS

Except for the biggest cities, life in urban and rural areas is fairly similar. There are libraries, youth clubs, entertainment complexes, and attractive restaurants in all the small towns and the villages. Most homes are occupied by one or two families, with front yards planted with flowers and with neat vegetable plots in the back.

Bulgarians are fond of their gardens. Whether they have to travel to the outskirts of the city to tend their plot in a communal garden or merely step out into their backyard, Bulgarians cultivate their gardens to perfection.

Thriving villages, especially those in the mountains in the south central and southeastern parts of the country, lost a great deal of their population when people started moving to the cities to work during the industrialization period. The cities, in turn, experienced severe housing shortages. To cope with this, the government started subsidizing housing projects. Today, most people in the large cities live in these government-built and unattractive buildings.

ENJOYING THE COUNTRY LIFE

The economic crises of the late 1990s were felt most strongly in the industrial sector and made the cost of urban living very expensive. As a result, many families left big cities for a more affordable lifestyle in the country. Life in the country is cheaper, less stressful, and healthier, and there are more local

A Bulgarian family gathers outside their rural home.

possibilities for enterprising individuals. As a result, Bulgarian villages and small towns are once again brimming with life.

Meanwhile, cities and their suburbs are witnessing the rebirth of the one-family home. New Bulgarian houses are solid, beautiful, and built to last with deep foundations, brick walls, and red-tiled roofs. When they build a home, most Bulgarians plan it so that a new floor for a future generation can be added on. This allows families to continue living in the extended-family arrangement that has been the basic way of life in Bulgaria for centuries.

EDUCATION IS KEY

Education is extremely important in Bulgarian society. The country has a comprehensive and strict educational system, with unique opportunities for study. Competitive examinations regulate access to education. The demand for good education at all levels is so high that even some of the new private schools, where families pay high tuition fees for the students, have introduced such entrance examinations.

Roma students attend class at their local school.

After 1989, secondary schools were created for students with different ethnic identities. For the first time, these students could learn two native languages, two cultures, and two religions—Bulgarian and their own native one. Two examples of ethnic schools are the Jewish school in Sofia and the Turkish school in the town of Kurdzhali. The idea of ethnic schools is based on the understanding that knowledge is the first step toward accepting ethnic differences and "otherness," an agreed-upon official educational policy of the country and a way to welcome the mixing of two different cultures.

Bulgarian education has a long democratic tradition. From the National Revival period of the nineteenth century onward, Bulgarians have taken pride in supporting their schools. Small mountain villages used to pool together their resources to send their most talented youths to prestigious schools in the cities or even abroad.

School attendance in Bulgaria is compulsory and free. High school dropout levels are very low. The current system of elementary, middle, and high school education, introduced in 1998, has twelve grades in which attendance is compulsory from ages seven though sixteen. Students attend elementary school for four years, basic (or middle) school for three years, and high school for three to five years, depending on the course of study. Students who perform well may continue their education at universities after passing the qualifying examinations.

Alternatively, vocational schools offer three years of practical training in a skilled trade. All high schools except vocational schools enable students to move on to higher education upon graduation. For adolescents with special talents, a number of high schools provide intensive advanced education in the arts, languages, or mathematics.

About 30 percent of Bulgarian students continue their education past the secondary level. In 2014 the country's literacy rate was 98.4 percent.

UNIVERSITIES   Colleges and universities train specialists for the professional job market. There are more than forty-two institutions of higher learning in Bulgaria, offering degrees at undergraduate and postgraduate levels. They include Sofia University and universities in Burgas, Blagoevgrad, Plovdiv, Ruse, Stara Zagora, Svishtov, Turnovo, and Varna. In 2012 there were more than 253,000 students enrolled in universities.

Saint Kliment Ohridski University in Sofia, founded in the nineteenth century, is the oldest university in Bulgaria.

INTERNET LINKS

http://www.afsusa.org/host-family/countries/bulgaria
This site gives a brief description of family life for Bulgarian teens.

http://www.country-data.com/cgi-bin/query/r-1924.html
Visit here for data and information about family life and the role of women in Bulgaria.

http://education.stateuniversity.com/pages/210/Bulgaria-EDUCATIONAL-SYSTEM-OVERVIEW.html
This site gives a detailed overview of the educational system in Bulgaria.

http://www.euroeducation.net/prof/bulgaco.htm
If you're interested in what opportunities Bulgarian students have after high school, this site is filled with information about universities, trade schools, and other options.

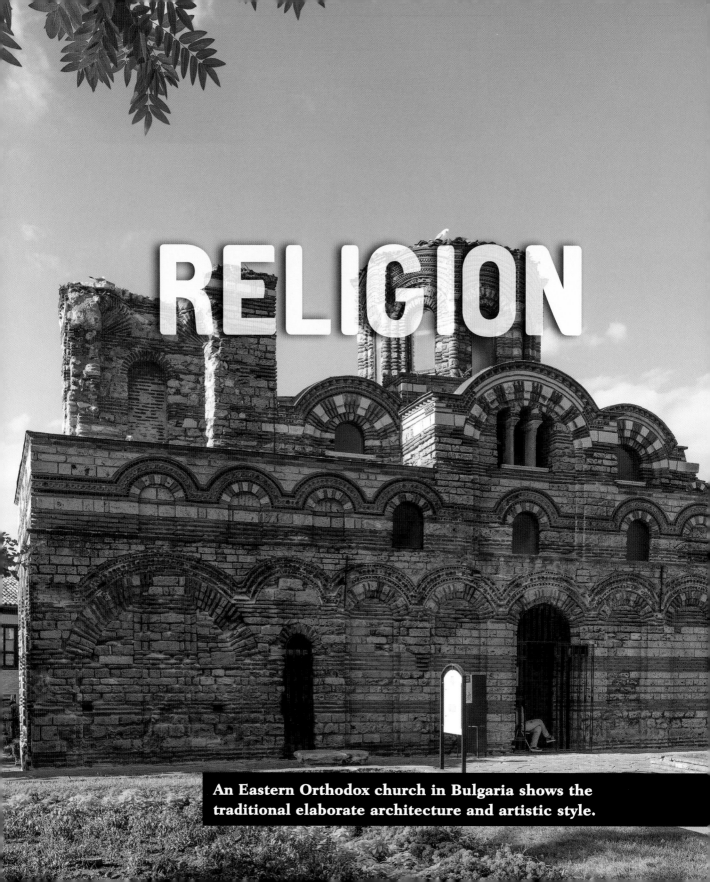

RELIGION

An Eastern Orthodox church in Bulgaria shows the traditional elaborate architecture and artistic style.

8

I N THE PAST, RELIGION WAS OF VITAL importance to most of Bulgaria's people. However, modern life and social changes have altered that. Today, religion is not a major part of life for most Bulgarians. Despite this, many Bulgarians still identify with a particular religion and its traditions, even if they do not practice that religion in their everyday lives.

The number of Orthodox priests in Bulgaria dropped from 3,312 in 1947 to 1,700 in 1985. During this time, many churches and monasteries were also taken over by the state and turned into museums.

A 2011 report showed that nearly 59.4 percent of Bulgaria's population is Orthodox Christian. This type of Christianity is also common in Greece, Russia, Romania, Serbia, Macedonia, Syria, Georgia, and in parts of Finland, Poland, the Czech Republic, Slovakia, Hungary, and Croatia.

Another 7.8 percent define themselves as Muslims. Less than 2 percent identify as Catholic, Protestant, Jewish, or Armenian Orthodox. About 3.7 percent identify as atheist, while 27.4 percent do not identify with a particular religion.

POLITICS AT WAR WITH RELIGION

Communism generally does not recognize religion and often forbids it completely. During the Communist era in Bulgaria, the Orthodox Church was pushed to the margins of social life. Religious knowledge was taken out of the state educational curriculum. The church was banned from its traditional activities, such as running orphanages and hospitals.

РЕЛИГИЯ-ЯД
БЕРЕГИ РЕБЯТ
ШКОЛА

This Communist-era poster proclaims, "Religion is poison," and was intended to warn Bulgarians away from organized religion.

Religious holidays and the rites of baptism, marriage, and burial were replaced by socialist holidays and rituals. Although the constitution of 1971 guaranteed freedom of religious beliefs and rituals, the state made it very clear to all students and government employees that attending religious services would damage their future and their careers.

Religious knowledge had been commonly passed on from one generation to another, but this practice declined after industrialization in the 1960s and 1970s caused a great many young people to move from their families in villages into new homes in cities. The constitution of 1971 also required parents to give their children a "Communist upbringing," and it stipulated that the education of youth "in a Communist spirit is the duty of the entire society." This requirement also discouraged parents from passing religious beliefs and rituals on to their children.

The sustained efforts of the state to have people follow an atheist way of life were by and large successful. The collapse of the Communist regime in 1989, however, led to a revival of Orthodox religious activities. It was no coincidence that the huge rallies of the anti-Communist opposition were held in the squares in front of city cathedrals. This choice of venue meant that the democratic movement symbolically connected to the Orthodox Church.

EASTERN AND WESTERN CONTROVERSY

For many centuries, the Orthodox Church was virtually unknown in the Western world. Although there have been numerous contacts between the

Orthodox, Roman Catholic, and Reformed Churches, the differences among them are still not clear to many people. In the East and the West, Christians believe in the Holy Trinity of the Father, the Son, and the Holy Spirit, and base their dogmas on the Old and New Testaments. However, the churches of the East and the West differ on certain controversial points. Eastern theology upholds the absolute equality of the Father, the Son, and the Holy Spirit, and believes that each entity is different in relation to the others. Western theology, on the other hand, emphasizes the unity of God, and that the Holy Spirit proceeds from the Father just as from the Son.

The heart of the controversy between the two churches concerns the administrative hierarchy. The Western side has a monarchical conception of the church, in which the pope has the authority to rule over the whole of Christendom. The Eastern side, on the other hand, sees Christendom as a community of self-governing churches, without needing to recognize papal supremacy.

THE HISTORICAL ROLE OF THE CHURCH

The Orthodox Church has played an important role in the building and survival of the Bulgarian nation. The Slavs and the Bulgars who founded the Bulgarian state in 681 CE had quite different belief systems, which raised obstacles to their integration. However, each of these peoples did believe in a pantheon of deities ruled by a mighty god of thunder, who was called Perun by the Slavic tribes and Tangra by the Bulgars. Bulgaria was converted to Christianity by Byzantine priests in the ninth century. Ever since, the Bulgarians have had their own national church that was equal with Constantinople's.

During the 860s, two brothers named Cyril and Methodius had a powerful effect on the Eastern Church in Bulgaria. In their everyday teachings, Cyril and Methodius used the common spoken Slavic language as well as their own Slavic translations of the scriptures, written in the new Cyrillic alphabet. These practices prevented cultural assimilation by the Byzantine Empire and gave the Bulgarian Church a strong identity.

After the fall of Bulgaria to the Turks, the independent Bulgarian Church came under the authority of the Greek patriarch in Constantinople. The

Statues of Cyril and Methodius near a Bulgarian Orthodox church.

National Revival movement, started within the church, gave the nation back its place in history. This movement gathered pace after the passionate assertion of Bulgarian historical identity by Father Paisiy Hilendarski, a monk from the Chilendar Monastery, in his *Slav-Bulgarian History*.

The first independent Bulgarian schools were opened in the monasteries. In 1870, the Turkish sultan issued a decree granting Bulgarians the right to organize a Bulgarian Orthodox Church. As the first Bulgarian national institution in the Ottoman Empire, the Orthodox Church played an important role in the movement for national liberation.

OTHER KEY RELIGIOUS GROUPS

MUSLIMS After Orthodox Christianity, Islam has the second-largest number of followers in Bulgaria, with three main Muslim groups: the Turks, Bulgarians, and Roma. The Turks have the largest numbers of believers, with 444,434 members as of 2011.

Most Muslims in Bulgaria are Sunnis, the form of the Muslim religion that became widespread during the Ottoman Empire. Sunni Muslims traditionally live in close communities, where they maintain a strong sense of ethnic and religious identity. Like the Orthodox Christians, the Muslims in Bulgaria had a difficult time under the Communist regime. Persecution was far more severe for the Muslims, since they were also under intense pressure to renounce their faith and to assimilate.

During the Communist era, mosques rapidly disappeared from the Muslim villages, with modern buildings taking their place. Pilgrimages to Mecca, one of the Five Pillars of Islam, became practically impossible. As a result, there was a general ignorance of the tenets of Islam. Muslims have been working since the collapse of Communism in 1989 to rebuild their faith in Bulgaria.

JEWS The Jews in Bulgaria were a well-organized religious community until World War II. At that time, most of the Jews were Sephardim, but there were also some Ashkenazim who came from countries north of the Danube. The Jews were governed by a central consistory, like a church council, and a chief rabbi in Sofia. Cities with a large concentration of Jews also had their own consistory and rabbi.

Muslims worship in a mosque in downtown Sofia.

Like many European nations, Bulgaria was overwhelmed by an influx of refugees fleeing war in Syria and other Middle Eastern countries. Many of these refugees are Muslim, and there are fears that some of them support ISIS and will commit terrorist acts in Bulgaria and other European nations. Despite its Muslim population, the Bulgarian government has been less than welcoming to migrants fleeing the Middle East.

Bulgarian police patrol along a barbed-wire fence built on the border of Bulgaria and Turkey to keep out migrants from the Middle East.

After the establishment of the state of Israel, a mass exodus in 1948–1949 left behind only three thousand to six thousand Jews, most of them in Sofia and largely nonbelievers. Today, the main synagogue in Bulgaria is in Sofia. Since 2009, the one hundredth anniversary of the synagogue in Sofia, there has been one rabbi, Josh Arens, serving there.

OTHER CHRISTIANS   The twenty thousand Bulgarian Armenians are mostly descendants of refugees from the persecution of Armenians in Turkey. They are adherents of the Armenian Gregorian Church. They are headed by a bishop who resides in Bucharest, Romania. The Armenian Church maintains close contacts with the Bulgarian Orthodox Church. In addition, Catholicism came to Bulgaria during the thirteenth and fourteenth centuries when Franciscan missionaries established communities in western Bulgaria.

The Protestant community is the smallest Christian group and the one with the most recent history. The first converts were made in the mid-nineteenth century by American Methodist and Congregationalist missionaries who came to southern Bulgaria.

Both Catholics and Protestants were treated harshly during the years after World War II because the Communists mistrusted their connections with Western democratic nations in Europe and North America. During the Communist era, pastors, priests, nuns, and lay believers were viewed as spies and dissidents. They faced many hardships, including prison and even death. However, there has been a marked revival among these religious groups, starting in the 1970s and continuing in the twenty-first century. Evangelical Protestants are the fastest-growing religious group in Bulgaria today, with more than six thousand members who practice their faith even though these denominations still face mistrust from many other religious and government groups.

Since the emergence of democracy in 1989, there has been a revival of religious life in Bulgaria. The Bulgarian Orthodox Church now has some 6.5 million members, with 2,600 parishes guided by 1,500 parish priests. It also runs 120 monasteries in Bulgaria with about 200 monks and nuns.

INTERNET LINKS

http://www.bulgarianembassy-london.org/index2.php?option=com_content&do_pdf=1&id=32
This website offers a brief overview of the Bulgarian Orthodox Church and its history.

http://countrystudies.us/bulgaria/26.htm
Here you can find information about the different religions in Bulgaria and the nation's reputation for religious tolerance.

http://flipfloppeople.com/Religions-in-Bulgaria-106
This site summarizes the basic facts about the major religions practicing in Bulgaria today.

http://www.muslimpopulation.com/Europe/Bulgaria/Islam%20in%20Bulgaria.php
This overview describes the Muslim population of Bulgaria, its history, and demographics.

A document declares Bulgaria's independence, written in traditional Bulgarian script.

FEW ELEMENTS ARE MORE IMPORTANT to a nation's identity than language. This is true in Bulgaria, where the Bulgarian language has played an important role in both defining and preserving national identity. Bulgarian is a Southern Slavic language, related to Slovenian, Serbian, and Croatian. Fewer than twenty words can be traced back to the tongue of the ancient Bulgars, which is believed to have been of Turanian origin. The main languages spoken in Bulgaria are Bulgarian, Turkish, Wallachian, Armenian, and Greek.

BULGARIAN is the official language of the nation. It is spoken by 76.8 percent of citizens. Bulgarian has absorbed many Turkish words as well as grammatical features of other non-Slavic Balkan languages. Bulgarian is taught in schools and is used in government and other official capacities.

TURKISH is spoken by many Muslims in the south-central and northeastern parts of Bulgaria, and by about 8 percent of the population

A man reads a book in a bookstore in Sofia.

overall. It is a Turanian language related to the tongue of the old Bulgars but is very different from modern Bulgarian. This language was brought to Bulgaria by the Turkish conquerors who came to Bulgaria from Central Asia in the fourteenth century.

WALLACHIAN is a dialect of Romanian and is spoken by a significant segment of the population inhabiting the northwest corner of Bulgaria as well as the narrow strip of about 100 miles (161 km) along the Danube River from the Serbian-Bulgarian border to the Black Sea.

ARMENIAN is an Indo-European language spoken by the descendants of the Armenian Holocaust refugees. In the early twentieth century, Armenians settled in Bulgaria west of the Black Sea. Over four million people in the former Soviet Union, Iraq, Lebanon, Syria, Iran, and Turkey speak this exotic language, which has its own alphabet.

GREEK is spoken by Bulgarian Greeks along the Black Sea coast and in the south of the country. It is written in a unique script, the basis for the Cyrillic alphabet used in Bulgaria, Macedonia, and Russia.

A LANGUAGE TO BE PROUD OF

The Bulgarians are extremely proud of their language. They were the first among the Slavic peoples to create a rich religious and secular literature. Additionally, it was the Slavic holy brothers Cyril and Methodius, and their disciple Saint Clement of Ohrid, whom medieval Europe had to thank for the

Cyrillic alphabet. Their invention of Slavic letters and translation of the scriptures into the spoken Slavic language was an outstanding cultural achievement.

Saints Cyril and Methodius had originally devised the Slav-Bulgarian alphabet for the purpose of establishing a Slavic church in Moravia (present-day Slovakia). Although their church mission collapsed, the alphabet system survived because some of their Slavic apostles found refuge in Bulgaria, where they spread the alphabet among the people.

The educational and creative work of these disciples brought forth a golden age of literature and culture in their new country. In the churches and at court, the Bulgarian language replaced Greek. The Cyrillic alphabet, along with Slavic liturgy, literature, and law, spread from Bulgaria to Serbia, Russia, and other lands.

Bulgarian became the international language of Slavic civilization, which spread cultural accomplishments and influences throughout the Balkans and northward to Russia. A number of Slavic peoples still use the Cyrillic script, with some minor variations to accommodate phonetic differences.

A hand-drawn chart shows the Slavic alphabet.

ALPHABET, GRAMMAR, AND DIALECTS

Bulgarian has an alphabet of thirty letters, with six vowels, two letters for composite diphthongs, twenty-one consonants, and one letter to indicate soft consonants. Although Bulgarian is a melodious language that is not difficult to pronounce, it has an extremely complicated system of grammar.

Although Bulgaria is a small country, there are considerable regional differences among the dialects spoken. These concern mainly the sounds of words, but there are also Bulgarian dialects with subtle variations in word choice and even some grammatical differences.

The Greek brothers Cyril and Methodius were experienced missionaries and church intellectuals who lived in the mid-ninth century. The younger brother, Constantine the Philosopher, who was renamed Cyril when he joined a monastery, was educated at the school for the children of the Byzantine imperial family. He had a gift for languages and held prestigious positions as professor of philosophy at the Magnaura Palace School and as librarian of the patriarchal church of Saint Sophia in Constantinople.

In their missionary and translating work, and as inventors of the script that was the precursor of the Cyrillic alphabet, the brothers worked wholeheartedly for the enlightenment of the Slavs. They bravely defended their cause in the Holy City of Rome, which did not always support their mission. Their work among the Slavs of Moravia antagonized the German clergy, who regarded Moravia as their missionary field. The two brothers were accused of heresy for not teaching Christianity in one of the three holy languages, which were Greek, Latin, or Hebrew.

As a result of the heresy accusation, Cyril and Methodius were summoned by the pope to account for their actions. On their way to Rome, they were drawn into a dispute with Venetian clergymen. It was then that Cyril formulated his defense of the use of the Slavic language in liturgy and learning.

SPEAKING WITH THE WHOLE BODY

Bulgarians may appear somewhat reserved, yet they often become very animated during conversations. They use their eyes, eyebrows, and hands to emphasize a point or to express approval or disagreement. When speaking, both men and women tend to make physical contact much more often than people in most Western cultures. They also stand closer together and chat in louder voices.

Perhaps most confusing to outsiders is the Bulgarian habit of shaking the head right to left to express agreement or compliance. Since this is the opposite of Western practice, it appears to Western onlookers that Bulgarians are always disagreeing with each other. Also, a Bulgarian gently nods his head up and down to signify "no," which is also the opposite of what people do in the West. "No" is also commonly expressed by an accompanying series of clicking sounds of the tongue. To muddle matters even more, there are Bulgarians who shake and nod their heads in the Western manner. On top of all this, the Greek minority shares with Bulgarians the same gestures for "yes" and "no," but the Greek word for "no" means "yes" in Bulgarian. Similarly, a waving finger may not signify a threat, but may merely draw attention to a point of importance. Actual disapproval is easily inferred from a string of loud clicking sounds and from raised eyebrows.

Bulgarians enjoy a lively conversation in the town square of Elhovo.

Bulgarians greet each other very warmly. It is common among members of both sexes to extend one or both hands to each other, and to exchange a kiss or three on the cheek. The number of kisses is always odd because even numbers are considered bad luck.

THE LANGUAGE OF NAMES

Bulgarians have three names—the given name, the father's name, and the family name, which can sometimes be the paternal grandfather's name. It is a common tradition to call children after their grandparents, and so the given name of the firstborn son differs from the family name only in its ending— for example, Georgi Georgiev, meaning Georgi's Georgi.

Variations on the grandparents' names are frequent. These may keep only the root or just a recognizable cluster of sounds. For example, a girl named Ralitza could be named after her grandmother Radka, or a boy named Miloslav could be named after his grandfather Milko.

The family name is the usual form of address at work, preceded by a polite Mr., Mrs., Miss, Doctor, or Professor. When Bulgarians talk to strangers, they invariably use the polite form of address. The formal "you" is appropriate for addressing business associates, unless there is a close working relationship. This is also the mandatory form of addressing one's teachers and professors, even when students and teachers have become friends in adulthood.

When a Bulgarian woman marries, she can adopt her husband's last name, retain her old family name, or combine the two in hyphenated form. Women who marry young usually opt for the traditional choice of adopting the husband's name. But female college graduates now often prefer to retain their family name or some form of it after marriage. Last names are especially useful for indicating the person's ethnic origin. Typically, last names have Slavic endings, except for some Jewish and Armenian names. Thus the family name derived from the Greek name Stavros has the masculine form of Stavrev and the feminine form of Stavreva. No Slavic endings are added to Jewish or Armenian family names.

Bulgarians pass time on a sunny day reading and talking at a sidewalk café.

PUBLIC CONVERSATIONS

Conversations in public can be quite lively and loud. People meet and discuss the events of the day, the political situation, or the latest neighborhood gossip. Shoppers in the marketplace chat as they buy food and other goods, while people gather in cafés and coffee shops. In public places like these, it is easy to strike up a conversation with a stranger. People also converse on public transportation, such as a long train trip. It is exciting to hear the Bulgarian language as people chatter about everything from their daily lives to the funniest and the most heartbreaking life stories. Language makes these connections possible and helps bring together the Bulgarian nation.

INTERNET LINKS

http://www.encyclopedia.com/people/philosophy-and-religion/saints/saints-cyril-and-methodius
This interesting article will help you learn more about Cyril and Methodius, and their importance to the Bulgarian language.

http://languageknowledge.eu/countries/bulgaria
This chart shows the different languages spoken in Bulgaria.

http://www.mastersportal.eu/articles/1019/bulgarian-language-all-you-need-to-know-about-bulgarian.html
This brief overview discusses Bulgaria's language, alphabet, and linguistic culture.

http://www.omniglot.com/writing/bulgarian.htm
Along with a short description of the Bulgarian language, this site includes the alphabet and audio clips of the spoken word.

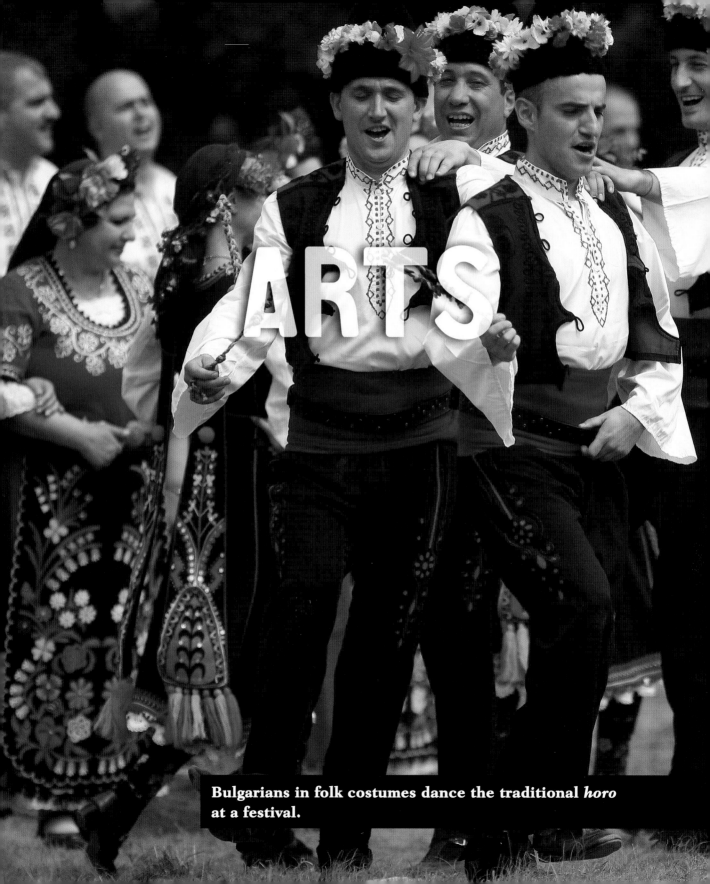

ARTS

Bulgarians in folk costumes dance the traditional *horo* at a festival.

10

THE ARTS ARE ONE OF THE MOST important ways that people express themselves. In Bulgaria, the history of the arts dates back to ancient times. The Thracians, Romans, ancient Greeks, Bulgars, and medieval Bulgarians all left traces of their unique artistic lives on the nation's culture. These artistic traditions can clearly be seen in the many ancient monuments discovered by archaeologists and historians. These monuments are treasure troves of ancient art, which can be as varied as a tomb filled with exquisite paintings and artifacts, Roman baths with mosaics, ancient theaters with stone columns, beautiful statues, and illuminated manuscripts.

A distinctive feature of Bulgarian arts is its strong democratic tradition. In other nations, painting and classical music developed because of sponsorship by the state or the monarchy. However, the long centuries of foreign rule in Bulgaria prevented these high art forms from developing. Additionally, the political ups and downs of the nation

A singer from Bulgaria performs in the Eurovision song contest, a popular singing competition.

have shaped its visual arts, theater, and literature. This is especially evident in a form of realistic art called socialist realism, which was promoted as the most advanced form of artistic expression during Communist rule.

TRADITIONAL FOLK MUSIC AND DANCE

Music has a rich and illustrious history in Bulgaria. Traditional Bulgarian music includes folk songs and choral chants in Old Bulgarian, which were created and used for church services. The main instruments for this type of music are the *gaida* (bagpipe) and the *kaval* (wooden flute).

Bulgarian folk music has unusual and complex harmonies, lively rhythms, and an irregular beat. It also varies dramatically from region to region. In the Rhodope Mountains, folk songs tend to be slow and sad, accompanied by low-pitched bagpipes. In Sofia, the tempo picks up, resulting in wild, fast tunes. In the Pirin Mountains, the harmonies often rise to unimaginably high pitches.

The folk dances of Bulgaria can be traced back to the long centuries of Ottoman rule. The best known of these dances is the *horo* (ho-RO), a lively circular dance where the dancers hold hands and swirl around to the wild rhythm of the music.

Also popular is the *ruchenitza* (rah-che-NI-tza), a competitive dance where the best dancers in the village challenge each other's stamina and imagination.

In the remote villages of the Strandja Mountains, in southeast Bulgaria, visitors can witness an unforgettable dance of very ancient origin. On May 21, the day of Saints Constantine and Helena, the local people light huge bonfires. At sunset, when the fires have turned to red-hot embers, the steady beat of drums and the drone of bagpipes signal that it is time for the dancing to begin.

Barefoot men and women, carrying priceless icons in their hands, circle around the embers in time to the fast rhythms. Then, as they raise the religious images high above their heads, they step into the fire. The dance is long and ecstatic. At the end, the dancers shake the ashes and the embers from their feet and step out unharmed.

These fire dancers are called the Nestinari. Their gift is handed down from generation to generation, inherited as a family tradition. Even so, not every family member has the gift. Performers believe they are protected by their patrons, Saint Constantine and Saint Helena, who trace a safe path in front of the dancers.

The country has many professional ensembles for folk music and dancing, which take these traditional art forms to world audiences. A number of Bulgarian composers, both new and old, have been influenced by Bulgarian folk tunes and have used them in their works. Among the nation's leading twentieth-century composers are Petko Stainov and Pancho Vladigerov.

TREASURES OF THE MEDIEVAL CHURCH

Throughout the country, elaborately decorated churches and monasteries preserve a wealth of Bulgarian medieval art. Bulgarians take great pride in the stunning frescoes adorning the thirteenth-century Boyana Church,

The Rila Monastery includes some of the most colorful and beautiful art in the world and has been named a UNESCO World Heritage site.

located in the Sofia suburb of Boyana. The Rila Monastery is equally famous for its wall paintings by Zakhari Zograph and other important icons painted between the fourteenth and nineteenth centuries. Also on display in Sofia's Alexander Nevsky Memorial Cathedral are over three hundred Orthodox iconic paintings, some a thousand years old.

Most Bulgarian icons date from the Ottoman period, when Christianity, once the stronghold of state power, became the faith of the oppressed. These small paintings were usually created on wooden panels and often feature stylized art in both vibrant and dark colors. Icons were also commonly used in daily devotions at home.

During the National Revival period, the Bulgarian icon became more expressive. Its distinctive features show an interest in human personality, dramatic detail, and landscape elements.

Icon painters, goldsmiths, wood carvers, and other artisans blended Islamic art with Western European styles and the Balkan art of icon making. They developed their own schools, each with a distinctive style. Bulgarian religious art of the eighteenth and nineteenth centuries shows an especially strong confidence in artistry.

EARLY BULGARIAN LITERATURE

The earliest Bulgarian literature can be traced to the ninth century, when Saints Cyril and Methodius created an alphabet for Old Bulgarian, which became the basis of the Old Church Slavonic language. This was a major literary language of Europe, and the Cyrillic alphabet and script were later adopted by Russia and Serbia.

Most of the Bulgarian writings produced between the ninth and the fourteenth centuries consisted of historical chronicles and translations of religious works. Some of the most important works were produced during the National Revival period in the nineteenth century. At that time, Father Paisiy's *Slav-Bulgarian History* became the handbook for the Bulgarian Enlightenment. Among the best-known writers of the past was the poet, novelist, and playwright Ivan Vazov, whose works detailed Bulgarian oppression under Ottoman rule. His writings defined much of the Bulgarian character and influenced many generations of Bulgarian writers.

A statue of Ivan Vazov, one of Bulgaria's most beloved writers.

ART MEETS POLITICS

Bulgaria has a strong theatrical tradition that has powerful connections to the political pulse of the nation. The first theatrical performances in Bulgaria took place at the popular library clubs during the middle of the nineteenth century. They were organized by schoolteachers and educators, and were intended to stir national consciousness and spur on the people to fight for independence and social justice.

When Russian leader Mikhail Gorbachev introduced perestroika, the program of liberalization and restructuring of the Soviet system, its spirit became a strong part of Bulgaria's theatrical and cinematic scenes.

Zakhari Zograph was one of the most talented painters from the Samokov school of iconographers. His secular and realist paintings in the early nineteenth century were among the most influential Bulgarian works of that time. Zakhari had no formal art education in European schools, but he studied Western engravings and paintings in his father's collection. He came from an artistic family, and his brother painted the scenes of the Apocalypse in the Rila Monastery.

Zakhari's frescoes adorn the walls of dozens of Bulgarian churches. He clearly drew inspiration from the image of the wheel of life, which he painted in the monasteries of Preobrazhenie and Troyan. His art shows his compulsion to fulfill his creative potential before the wheel lowered him into the open jaws of the monster.

Zakhari's frescoes illustrate dramatic biblical scenes, but they also depict the daily lives of ordinary people of the Bulgarian towns and villages. The highest compliment to his talent was an invitation to paint in the cathedral church on holy Mount Athos.

Playwrights, scriptwriters, and film producers worked out a symbolic language that eluded government censorship. Their works, complete with philosophic and moral parables, allowed them to launch attacks on the regime of the day in the form of bitter political satires. The cinemas and theaters of Bulgaria became the first venues where government propaganda gave way to free thinking.

In modern times, the theater continues to be a popular form of entertainment. Audiences enjoy modern foreign dramas and both traditional and contemporary Bulgarian plays, including those by noted Bulgarian playwright Ivan Vazov and poet Peyo Yavorov.

ARTISTS BREAK FREE

Cultural policies under Communist rule enforced an official culture based on Communist ideology. Between 1977 and 1981, state support was exceptionally generous, but artistic production was tightly controlled, with severe penalties for transgression.

The government suppressed freedom of speech and controlled public art and literature with rigid censorship. Fortunately, intellectual and political dissent never entirely disappeared from artistic life.

In the 1980s, cultural funding from the state dwindled to almost nothing. Suddenly freed from censorship but with no financial support, Bulgarian artists started forming small collectives to share production costs. These groups included the Society for Art in Action and the City Group.

Artists were willing to experiment and to be politically involved. They worked with unconventional materials, exhibited in unusual places, and integrated exhibition with performance. Totalitarian controls over art finally

Actors rehearse a scene from a play. Theater is very popular in Bulgaria.

An archaeologist holds up an ancient drinking vessel from the excavation of a Thracian royal tomb in Sofia.

ended with the fall of Communism in 1989, and artistic expression has since reemerged as a vibrant force.

One of the most outstanding twenty-first-century Bulgarian artists is Christo, a sculptor known worldwide for his technique of wrapping famous buildings and monuments in fabric and plastic. His artworks include *The Gates* in New York City's Central Park and *Floating Piers* on Lake Iseo in Italy.

DIGGING INTO THE PAST

Bulgaria is a paradise for archaeologists. It seems that excavations are always going on, and there is a wealth of material to discover, thanks to the various ancient civilizations that were part of Bulgaria's history. Scientists are especially excited at what they find underneath Bulgarian cities that rest atop ancient foundations. Some of these archaeological discoveries are so amazing and beautiful that they have been exhibited all over the world.

KAZANLUK TOMB Two thousand years ago, Roman legions subdued the thriving civilization of the Thracians. The tomb of a Thracian tribal chief, built in the third century BCE, was discovered in 1944 in the city of Kazanluk. The leader was buried along with all the finery and decorated weapons that he might need in the afterlife. This tomb beautifully demonstrates the craftsmanship of the Thracian masters. Perfectly preserved frescoes include human and animal figures painted in such vibrant colors that they look as if they are about to step off the wall. The chief and his wife are portrayed as touching each other tenderly.

PLOVDIV THEATER There are so many ancient artifacts in the center of Plovdiv that people hardly dare to dig foundations for new buildings for fear of damaging valuable ancient relics. One such rare find, on the outskirts of the Old Town, is a huge theater built in Roman times. The structure is very well preserved, from the stage to the most distant row of seats. Today Bulgarians can enjoy plays in this theater under the summer sky, overlooking the historical hills of ancient Plovdiv.

The Roman theater in Plovdiv is still in use today.

INTERNET LINKS

https://blazingbulgaria.wordpress.com/music-of-bulgaria
This site has a comprehensive look at the many styles of Bulgaria's music, as well as video and audio clips of different styles.

http://bnr.bg/en/post/100696132/national-gallery-of-arts-presents-ivan-mrkvicka-and-modern-bulgaria-painting
This website takes a visual and informational look at one of modern Bulgaria's most famous artists.

http://www.visitplovdiv.com/en/node/522
Take a virtual tour of the ancient Plovdiv theater and learn about its history at this fascinating website.

LEISURE

These elderly women enjoy a friendly visit after a day's work.

L EISURE TIME IS IMPORTANT TO most people, and it seems that the harder people work, the more they value time to play and relax. However, the idea of leisure time has a bit of a twist in Bulgaria, where people value getting things done. This belief is clearly seen in an old Bulgarian saying: "It is fine to work in vain, but not to sit around in vain." After a long day at work, Bulgarians do not kick off their shoes and relax. Instead, they busy themselves with tasks around the house.

In the countryside, when Bulgarian women get together, they are likely to bring some work along with them. A leisurely afternoon with friends does not include sitting around and doing nothing! Instead, friends help each other with a knitting or embroidery project, or work together on the cooking for an upcoming celebration.

Meanwhile, men often spend their leisure time making wine and brandy. Bulgarians are convinced that there is no better wine than their own, produced from homegrown grapes and fruits of their own labor.

WORKING FOR THE WEEKEND

Making wine is a favorite weekend communal activity in the fall. Friends gather together to help, taste each other's products, tell stories, and sing

11

Bulgarians are known for their sense of humor. When things get tough for Bulgarians, they respond with an avalanche of jokes. The most popular jokes ridicule and highlight the shortcomings of Bulgarians' national character or the inadequacies and follies of ruling politicians.

A Bulgarian man checks his tomato crop. Bulgarians find space to garden, even in large cities and towns.

songs. The men may also indulge in a game of cards or backgammon.

Gardening is another popular weekend pastime. Gardening is considered a hobby, rather than work. Residents in small towns and villages have little vegetable gardens in their backyards, while those in the cities travel to the outskirts or to summer houses in the countryside to tend their gardens.

Bulgarians are perfectionists when it comes to gardening. Along the Black Sea coast, little family vineyards get just as much loving attention as the largest ones in the land.

A NATION OF COFFEE DRINKERS

There are few things Bulgarians love more than coffee, and this beverage is an important part of the nation's leisure. Bulgarians drink coffee at all hours of the day and especially in the late afternoon. On weekends, city dwellers stroll along streets dotted with small cafés, each with its own distinct atmosphere and faithful clientele.

Some of the cafés are like social clubs, where lawyers, actors, university professors, writers, artists, and people in the film industry each have their chosen corners.

If they are not visiting a coffeehouse, Bulgarians love to visit friends and relatives. They take flowers and perhaps a bottle of homemade wine for their hosts. However, as everyday lives have become busier, these visits usually occur because of a special occasion. These celebrations include important festive days such as birthdays and name days, or the days devoted to patron saints in the Eastern Orthodox Christian calendar. It is a mark of social prestige to be remembered by a lot of people on these days.

VACATIONS AT THE BEACH OR IN THE MOUNTAINS

In July and August, most Bulgarians leave their towns for vacations. School is out, theaters and concert halls close for the summer, and cities grow hot and dusty. Families with relatives living on farms in the countryside may visit and help with the fieldwork during the summer months.

The most popular vacationing places are the mountains and the Black Sea coast. Their numerous resorts offer camping sites, shelters, and chalets for people of all tastes and incomes.

Both foreign and Bulgarian tourists enjoy visiting the beautiful beaches of the Black Sea coast.

The Black Sea coast, with its warm clear water and sandy beaches, adjacent forests and river deltas, and spectacular vegetation, is by far the best-loved vacation area for most Bulgarians. They go there to relax, camp, swim, fish, and row. But those who live by the sea usually spend their vacations in the mountains to enjoy their green and cool landscape, crystal-clear lakes, modern resorts, and well-marked hiking trails.

SKIING AND OTHER SPORTS

The Bulgarian mountains are also popular in the winter months. The biggest mountain resorts are in the Rila and Rhodope Mountains and at Mount Vitosha. Good snowfalls and snow cover that lasts up to 180 days of the year provide excellent skiing conditions.

Even the city dwellers in Sofia are able to enjoy skiing. The city is located at the foot of Mount Vitosha, only a half-hour drive from excellent ski and toboggan runs.

Other popular sports are soccer and basketball. No matter whether they are from a city or a small village, little boys learn to kick a soccer ball almost as soon as they can walk.

Bulgarian fans cheer their team at a soccer match.

Soccer games are always well attended, and the country's soccer players are popular celebrities. One of the nation's proudest sports moments occurred when the Bulgarian soccer team defeated Germany in the quarterfinals of the 1994 World Cup. The Bulgarian people celebrated with tremendous joy and pride, and a spectacular rally was held in Sofia.

Basketball is a recent arrival in Bulgaria and is more popular in the cities than in the country. Both girls and boys enjoy playing this game. Other favorite sports include volleyball, rowing, rhythmic gymnastics, track events, wrestling, and weightlifting. Generations of Bulgarian athletes have excelled at these sports in international competitions such as the Olympics.

A LOVE OF READING

Bulgarians love to read. The daily newspapers became everybody's favorite reading material for about two years after democratic changes began, as Bulgarians tried to keep up with the rapid cultural, social, and political developments. At the time, newspapers were so popular that it was very difficult to find a leading newspaper after 8 a.m. This frenzied hunger for real news, however, has abated. Bulgarians have also had a long history of

NEWS VIA THE INTERNET

Although Bulgarians still turn to newspapers, television, and radio as a source of news, they are also using the internet in increasing numbers. Between 2000 and 2014, the number of internet users in Bulgaria increased from 430,000, or about 5 percent of the population, to 4,083,950, or almost 57 percent.

reading novels, short fiction, and poetry. They read everywhere: on the train, on the bus, and at home in the evenings. Public libraries and bookstores are always full of people. When the weather is good, book vendors display their goods to crowds in the city centers.

Bulgarians bring their love of reading everywhere, even to the beach.

SLY PETER AND BAI GANYU

Bulgarians are fond of telling stories. Their favorite characters are sly peasants who are not too polished but daring and witty. Two such enduring figures are Sly Peter, who was created 1,300 years ago, and Bai Ganyu, who made his first appearance in 1895.

Sly Peter is adept at outwitting everybody, especially his social superiors and, at times, even himself. One story shows Sly Peter cleverly insulting the *chorbadjia*, the richest man in the village. Sly Peter and the chorbadjia were in a public bath. As soon as the chorbadjia finished his bath, he wound a sheet around himself and conceitedly asked, "Peter, seeing me as I am, nearly naked, how much do you estimate I'm worth?"

There is a city in Bulgaria that has an international reputation for laughing at its own citizens. It is Gabrovo, an important industrial center in the heart of Bulgaria. It boasts the world's first House of Humor and Satire. This museum, which opened in 1974, contains extensive exhibitions of humorous items.

The Festival of Humor and Satire started in Gabrovo in 1965 and has been held there every year since. "The world," the people of Gabrovo say, "has survived because it has laughed."

Here are a few typical jokes and anecdotes that poke fun at the slyness and stinginess of Gabrovo's citizens:

A young man told his father he wanted to become a heart specialist. "You fool!" cried his father. "Better study dentistry. Man has got one heart, but thirty-two teeth!"

Two Gabrovo drivers met on a narrow bridge, but neither would back up, in order not to waste fuel. One took out a newspaper and began to read, thinking the other would soon get fed up and back up. But the other driver got out, sat down on the hood of his car, and said, "After you've read the paper, can I borrow it?"

When entertaining guests on a name day, Gabrovo citizens put two or three uncracked nuts on top of a heap of nutshells, both for the sake of economy and in order to let people think that many guests have visited the name-day celebrant.

When renting rooms, people in Gabrovo always make sure that they get a window near a lamppost, so that they can make use of that light and not have to switch on their own lights at night.

"Hum." Sly Peter thought for a moment. "You're worth ten Turkish pennies."

"You fool!" The chorbadjia was angry. "Why, the sheet alone costs ten Turkish pennies!"

"I know," Sly Peter said calmly. "That's why I said ten Turkish pennies."

Bai Ganyu was originally a smart and ruthless peasant who was created by a journalist named Aleko Konstantinov. To keep pace with the modern world, Bulgarians have wittily transformed Bai Ganyu the peasant into Ganev the aspiring engineer, who shamelessly boasts of Bulgarian achievements in science and technology. He tends to say the wrong things, yet some of his blunders are telling comments that are clever put-downs of his international competitors.

One story tells of an international fair of new technologies. The Russians exhibited a clock with a little bird that came out on the hour crying loudly, "Lenin! Lenin!" But engineer Ganev got the better of the Russians by exhibiting a very similar clock. Only instead of the bird, it was a figure of Lenin who popped out, crying, "Cuckoo! Cuckoo!"

Another story of the conference features an American representative who brags that cellular phones and pagers had long become outdated in the United States. Instead, he said, Americans now use a tiny implant in their fingernail to send and receive information.

The Japanese representative claimed that they too had a similar device— but implanted in the tooth. At this point, engineer Ganev burped loudly but was quick to say, "I'm sorry, I just received a fax."

INTERNET LINKS

https://sites.google.com/site/karavansarays/bulgarian-folklore
This site has many examples of Sly Peter jokes.

http://mycountrybg.blogspot.com/2010/01/bulgarian-sports.html
This writer has created a firsthand account of Bulgaria's most popular sports and athletes.

http://www.onlinenewspapers.com/bulgaria.htm
This site has links to Bulgaria's major newspapers.

http://splitsider.com/2011/02/welcome-to-gabrovo-bulgarias-comedy-capital-and-favorite-punchline
This lengthy article features the story of Gabrovo as well as several examples of its jokes and humor.

FESTIVALS

Red and white decorations celebrate the holiday of Baba Marta.

12

FESTIVALS ARE AN IMPORTANT PART of Bulgaria's national heritage and a way to keep alive traditions of the past and honor important people, both past and present. Bulgaria's festivals have many different origins that show influences on the nation's history and culture.

Some of Bulgaria's holidays are Christian, some have pagan origins, and others commemorate Bulgarian historical events. There are many ways to celebrate. Some festivals include indoor activities where families and close friends gather together to feast and chat. Others are celebrated outdoors in city squares and village schoolyards, in vineyards, or at the beach. Even the festival dates are subject to change. Some festivals have fixed dates, while others do not. Some festivals even go on for longer than a day.

CHANGING INDEPENDENCE DAY

Under Communist rule, the Bulgarian national independence holiday was celebrated on September 9. On that day in 1944, eight months before the end of World War II in Europe, the Soviet army reached the capital, Sofia, in its advance toward Berlin. September 9, 1944, was therefore the first day of Bulgaria's socialist era. That day used to be celebrated in the grandiose style of Communist governments, with students and employees parading in huge groups in front of red-draped platforms, and with important members of the Communist Party being honored by the cheers of the people.

National Holidays

March 3	*The Liberation of Bulgaria (independence from the Ottoman Empire)*
May 1	*Labor Day*
May 24	*Day of Letters (celebrates Bulgarian education and culture, and the Cyrillic alphabet and Bulgarian press)*

Winter Holidays

December 25–27	*Christmas*
January 1	*Vassilyovden (Saint Vassil's Day)*
January 6	*Yordanovden (Epiphany)*
January 7	*Ivanovden (Saint John the Baptist's Day)*
January 18	*Atanasovden (Saint Athanasius's Day)*

Pre-Spring Holidays

February 14	*Trifon Zarezan (Day of the Vineyards)*
February	*(Sunday) Zagovezni (Shrovetide)*
March 1	*Baba Marta*
March	*(Saturday) Todorovden (Saint Todor's Day)*

Spring Holidays

March/April	*(Sunday) Easter*
May 6	*Gergyovden (Saint George's Day)*
May 21	*Saints Constantine and Helena's Day*

Fall Holidays

October 26	*Dimitrovden (Saint Dimitri's Day)*
November	*Day of the Souls*

After the collapse of Communism, Bulgarians recognized the need for a national holiday that would celebrate much more than a triumph of some political power. The new date picked was March 3, the day of the signing of the San Stefano peace treaty after the Russian-Turkish Liberation War of 1877—1878. This treaty reestablished the Bulgarian state after five centuries of Ottoman rule. March 3 became a fitting symbol of the day when Bulgaria's dreams of national liberty and unity came true.

BABA MARTA AND THE COMING OF SPRING

One of the most cheerful Bulgarian holidays is the day of Baba Marta, March 1. The name Marta means the month of March. According to Bulgarians, March is a "female month," since its weather changes as fast as the mood of "old Grandma Marta."

Early on the morning of Baba Marta day, Bulgarians tie little red and white tassels on each other or pin them on their coats with a wish for health, vigor, and happiness. These red and white decorations are called *martenitzi* (mahr-tay-NI-tzi). In the countryside people tie these tassels on domestic animals and fruit trees. The red and the white colors symbolize the blood of the new life that is awakening in the snow-covered country.

Children and adults wear the martenitzi in anticipation of spring, which is said to arrive with the storks from the south. When the first stork is sighted, Bulgarians take off their tassels and tie them onto a blossoming tree.

HONORING EDUCATION

In an old tradition, Bulgarians celebrate May 24 as the Day of Letters. This holiday was created by a teacher back in the days of Ottoman rule in the 1800s and was embraced with joy and pride by schoolchildren and their parents. Many of the parents were illiterate but harbored dreams of seeing their children educated and making a better life for themselves.

The Day of Letters is an exciting holiday, particularly for children who have just learned to read and write. On this day, the entire Bulgarian nation honors the apostles Cyril and Methodius and shows their love and gratitude to their disciples who founded the first schools in Bulgaria. The holiday also honors the teachers, educators, writers, journalists, actors, musicians, and artists of modern Bulgaria. On the Day of Letters, schoolchildren take flowers to their teachers and weave wreaths of ivy and flowers to place around portraits of Cyril and Methodius.

ANCIENT FESTIVAL TRADITIONS

Other festivals have origins in ancient religious or pagan traditions. These holidays include Christmas, the January winter festivals, spring festivals, Easter, harvest holidays, and the Day of the Souls. Christian meaning is often interwoven with ancient pagan rites.

The Christmas holidays go on for twelve days. They begin with Ignazhden (ig-NAHZH-dayn) on December 20 when, according to Bulgarian folklore, Mary felt her first birth pangs. On Christmas Eve, the last day of the Orthodox fast (November 15 to December 24), Bulgarian families gather around the table for the last vegetarian and nondairy meal of the season. Orthodox Christmas lasts three days, from December 25 to 27, and religious rituals are supplemented by carnival-like folk festivities. In the evenings, groups of young men go from house to house, singing Christmas songs and blessing the hosts.

Children hold *survachkas* as they visit family and friends on New Year's Day.

A similar tradition, called *survakane* (or *survaki*), is observed on the morning of New Year's Day, when children visit their extended family and close friends and neighbors to wish them health and prosperity. They playfully "beat" the elders on the back with a dogwood branch that has been tied with a handkerchief and other decorations, such as dried plums and popcorn. In return, the youngsters receive fruit, candy, and money. The dogwood, *survachka* (soor-VAHCH-kah), is chosen both for its sturdiness and because it is the first tree to blossom in the spring.

EARLY SPRING HOLIDAYS

Holidays in February and March anticipate the regeneration of new life in the spring. Although most of these holidays conform to the Christian Orthodox

calendar, they have the distinct flavor of pagan times. On Trifon Zarezan, the Festival of the Vineyards, the vines are trimmed in a mood of cheerful celebration and wine drinking. Cleansing rituals that are supposed to banish evil powers mark Zagovezni.

This is carnival time in some parts of the country. On one day, men put on festive clothes, huge elaborate masks, and cowbells, then dance their way through village streets, chasing away evil spirits.

The Easter holidays are preceded by Lent and a three-day strict fast for the most devout Orthodox Christians. These observances end in the elaborate church services and rituals that mark the week of Christ's Passion on the cross and his resurrection. For centuries, Easter has been the most important holiday for the Eastern Orthodox Christians.

One of the most beloved activities of Easter is dyeing hard-cooked eggs. This event is traditionally held on the eve of Good Friday. The first egg is

A Bulgarian wears a traditional mask to chase away evil spirits during the festival of Zagovezni.

Beautifully dyed eggs are a traditional part of a Bulgarian Easter celebration.

always dyed red and is then put under the family icon, where it remains until Easter Sunday. The next egg is dyed green, the color associated with spring and Saint George, whose day falls shortly after Easter, on May 6. Other colors are also used, and some eggs may be elaborately painted with designs. The eggs are kept until Easter morning, when people rap their own egg against someone else's. The last person to have an unbroken egg is said to be blessed with a good year. The whole family gathers around the table for a traditional breakfast of eggs and braided Easter breads, richly decorated with almonds and raisins.

CELEBRATING LIFE AND DEATH

Although the springtime holidays are associated with the names of various saints, they have a strong undercurrent of ancient pagan rites. These celebrations are wild and boisterous, and entire villages go out into the fields or the village square to dance. A number of rituals are dedicated to young people and to nature.

One of the biggest May holidays is Saint George's Day, the Day of the Shepherd. It is a true regional festival in the stockbreeding parts of the country, where people go to the mountains for games and dancing, and to feast on whole roasted lambs.

In the fall, there are harvest festivals and rituals commemorating the dead. The day of Saint Dimitar deserves special mention, as it marks the end of the agricultural cycle that began on Saint George's Day. Bulgarians observe the Day of the Souls, or Zadushnitza, by making a traditional dish of puffed wheat and some of the favorite cakes and candies of their deceased relatives. An important part of this festival has entire families visiting the cemeteries, where they place flowers on the graves of their loved ones and distribute the prepared food.

Holidays such as these show the strong connection Bulgarians have to traditions celebrated since ancient times and the power these festivals have over the nation's culture and beliefs. They also show the strong link to family, even family members who have passed away years before.

INTERNET LINKS

http://easteuropeanfood.about.com/od/bulgarianeasterntradition/a/How-Bulgarians-Celebrate-Easter.htm
Learn about the traditions of Holy Week and Easter in Bulgaria at this comprehensive site.

http://www.iexplore.com/articles/travel-guides/europe/bulgaria/festivals-and-events
This website provides information and photos of Bulgaria's major festivals and celebrations.

http://www.visitbulgaria.net/en/pages/official_holidays.html
This site has a complete list of Bulgaria's holidays.

FOOD

Bulgarians enjoy a delicious spread of vegetarian foods during the Christmas holiday.

13

ALL OVER THE WORLD, THE LOVE OF good food brings people together, and Bulgaria is no different. Nothing is more important than sharing a meal with loved ones. Although juggling the pace of modern life and the fact that young people have moved away from their homes for new lives in urban areas, families try very hard to have at least one daily meal together. They work mealtimes around the schedules of parents who have to work and children who attend school to create a time for everyone to gather around and share a good meal.

Both men and women love to cook, eat, and talk about food. There is food at every important occasion, whether it is a party, a celebration, or a commemoration of the dead. Even casual visitors to a Bulgarian home will be given something to eat, and if they are houseguests, they will get three excellent meals a day.

MEALS BIG AND SMALL

Lunch is traditionally the biggest meal of the day. It includes some kind of vegetable or meat soup, a main course of a pork, veal, or chicken dish with vegetables (often with a small salad on the side), and dessert. The meal is usually washed down with a glass of wine, which may be diluted with club soda. Teenage children are allowed to have a glass of light wine with their meals. Bulgarians do not see any harm in allowing young people to drink. They believe that if their children are taught to drink in moderation during a good meal, they are unlikely to abuse alcohol in the future.

Of course, nonalcoholic drinks are popular too. Favorite nonalcoholic drinks include various fruit nectars and juices and diluted yogurt. Desserts may be sweet pastries made with sugar syrup or honey, compotes of dried or preserved fruit cooked in syrup, or puddings.

BREAKFAST AND SUPPER On weekdays, breakfast is usually a hurried affair. Everyone in the house will simply grab a cup of tea or coffee and a piece of toast before they dash out of the house to work or school. Leisurely breakfasts are reserved for the weekend. A weekend breakfast might include pancakes, a warm cheese-and-egg pastry, or French toast with honey.

Bulgarian suppers are a treasured way to relax at the end of the day. This meal is lighter than lunch. It starts with a fresh salad or an appetizer of pickled vegetables, and a light drink called an aperitif. The most popular aperitifs include *rakia* (rah-KI-yah), the local grape or plum brandy, and *mastika* (mahs-TI-kah), an aniseed-based brandy that tastes like licorice. These drinks are slightly chilled and sipped slowly. The main course is usually a meat dish, followed by a light dessert, such as fresh fruit or a compote.

MEALTIME MANNERS

Bulgarians make sure to place all cutlery, condiments, and food, except dessert, on the table at the beginning of the meal. Once everyone is seated, nobody wants to get up again. In fact, it is considered impolite to interrupt the meal to ask for something not already there.

Wolfing down one's food without commenting on its taste is also considered rude. People are expected to keep up an easy conversation at mealtimes and to leave nothing uneaten on their plates. Asking for an extra serving is much appreciated and regarded as a compliment to the chef. A good lunch is often followed by a nap in the afternoon.

Bulgarians are meticulous about the use of a knife and fork, but they sometimes eat fish or chicken with their fingers. Napkins are used to wipe one's mouth at the end of each course or before taking a drink and are rarely spread across a person's lap.

CHANGING SEASONS, CHANGING MEALS

Bulgarians use seasonal ingredients to their full potential. Meat consumption, especially of pork and poultry, increases substantially in the winter months. Stews and hearty soups, using all parts of the animal or bird, are common dishes at these times of year. Sizzling pork chops or pork stews with canned vegetable sauces or sauerkraut are favorites, with an accompanying bottle or two of wine.

Homemade yogurt is eaten every day by people in Bulgaria.

A DAY AT THE MARKET

Lively outdoor markets in the cities are open year-round, but the most fascinating time to shop is on a Saturday in the fall. On these days, stallholders travel as much as 200 miles (320 km) away to sell their wares in the cities.

All manner of goods and fresh produce can be found at the markets, including live birds, lamb in season, fresh fruit and vegetables, honey, fish, flowers, and nuts. Shoppers can also find handicrafts, homespun woolen yarn, or hand-knit sweaters.

Market day starts at seven in the morning, and by six in the evening most stallholders are packing up and getting ready to go. Bulgarians are not accustomed to haggling, so the only time customers might get a real bargain is in the late afternoon when vendors are in a hurry to go home and are willing to negotiate.

A favorite aperitif in the cold winter months is *greyana rakia* (GRAY-an-nah rah-KI-yah), a plum or grape brandy heated with honey in a copper pot and served in tiny, thick cups.

Spring is the time to enjoy lamb with the first green vegetables, such as dock, spinach, and green onions. The summer diet is lighter and mostly vegetarian, using lots of fresh fruits and vegetables.

Yogurt makes an appearance at almost every meal. It is usually made from cow's milk, but yogurt from sheep's milk is a much-sought-after delicacy. From the age of three months onward, most Bulgarians have yogurt every day. Unlike Westerners, Bulgarians rarely mix yogurt with fruit or nuts.

Vine growing and wine production have a very long history in Bulgaria, starting in Thracian times. Together with beer and the local brandy known as rakia, wine is one of the most popular alcoholic beverages in the country. Bulgaria has five distinct viticultural regions: the Danubian Plain (north Bulgaria), the Black Sea (east Bulgaria), the Rose Valley (sub-Balkan), the Thracian lowlands (south Bulgaria), and the Struma River valley (southwest Bulgaria).

The quality of Bulgarian wine speaks for itself. Local wines such as Gumza, Dimiat, Pamid, Muscat, Misket, Mavrud, and Melnik are well known to connoisseurs all over the world. South Bulgaria is noted for its red wines, while North Bulgaria is recognized for its fine white ones. The Black Sea region, with Burgas, Pomorie, and Varna as its three main centers, is where 30 percent of all vines are cultivated. Melnik, in southwest Bulgaria, is a region famed for its full-bodied red wine.

Bulgarians love their wine so much that they celebrate Trifon Zarezan, or Saint Trifon's Day, on February 14. This holiday is dedicated to Saint Trifon, the patron saint of the vineyards and a symbol of fertility. On this day, vine growers hold vine-trimming ceremonies and perform rituals, celebratory songs, and dances as part of the festivities. This tradition dates back to the ancient Thracians and is not celebrated anywhere else in the world.

Certain foods are available only briefly, when they are in season. These dishes include lamb and most fresh fruits and vegetables. A shepherd's specialty from the Rhodope Mountains, called *kotmach* (kot-MAHCH), deserves special mention. The pungent cheese is made from sheep's milk only in the month of August, when grazing pastures have dried out and the sheep are nearing the end of their lactation period. Only at this time is the sheep's milk dense enough to be suitable for kotmach.

Bulgarians eat a lot of bread. A family of four goes through a 2-pound (1-kilogram) loaf or more within a day. They like their bread fresh and buy it daily. Bread is rarely baked at home, except for traditional New Year pita bread or the braided Easter breads. A slice of warm, heavy, crusty bread topped with feta cheese and slices of tomato is popular all year round.

Bulgarians roast lambs over a fire to create a traditional and tasty dish.

LOCAL VARIATIONS

Bulgarian cuisine reflects many different influences. It may include meats or be vegetarian or based on dairy products. Regional cuisines may recall Russian or central Asian influences, or the cooking of neighboring Yugoslavia and Romania. There are likely to be more pronounced differences in cooking within the regions of Bulgaria than when crossing national borders in the Balkans.

In the plains north of the Balkan Mountains, marinating food is a popular technique. Northern Bulgarian cuisine often uses finely ground meats. Popular dishes include a layered pastry with rice and meat filling, and baked sweet red peppers stuffed with beans.

Residents of the Black Sea coast and those living along the Danube enjoy a variety of fresh fish. Bulgarians like their seafood simple—grilled or deep-fried with a touch of lemon. On holidays, they may enjoy baked fish stuffed with finely chopped tomatoes, onions, chili peppers, and nuts.

Traditional cooking in the Rhodope Mountains is probably the healthiest regional cooking in the country. It rarely involves frying and uses very little oil, which is usually added to the food only when it has been cooked for some time. Rhodope meals include lots of garlic, nuts, and dairy products, and are examples of simple and natural cooking at its best. The best-known specialty from the Rhodope is *cheverme* (chay-vayr-MAY), or a whole lamb roasted on a spit and served with honey and a seasonal salad. Cheverme is traditionally cooked outdoors for big family holidays or for town or village festivals.

In the Thracian Plain bordering on the Rhodope area, cooking methods are very similar to those in Greece. Vegetables, olive oil, and spices are favorite ingredients of meals in this region. Meals are often cooked in several stages. Meats and vegetables are first lightly sautéed, then stewed or baked, and finally topped off with a sauce. The dish of rolled-up grape leaves stuffed with meat and rice known as *lozovi sarmi* (LO-zo-vi sahr-MI) is served with a yogurt sauce. This same dish is popular in Greece, where it goes by the name *dolmas*. It is easy to see how national borders are not important when it comes to enjoying a good meal!

INTERNET LINKS

http://www.findbgfood.com/bgmeals.htm
This site gives a quick overview of Bulgarian dishes, with links to many recipes.

http://www.findbgfood.com/rakia.htm
This site explains how rakia is made and why it is such an important part of Bulgarian meals.

http://www.mydestination-bulgaria.com/usefulinfo/traditional-food-in-bulgaria
The photos and information on this site provide an excellent and tasty overview of Bulgaria's traditional food.

TARATOR

This traditional Bulgarian soup is served cold and is a tasty treat on a hot day.

4 cups plain yogurt
1 cup water
Large cucumber, peeled and finely chopped
1 garlic clove, pressed
½ bunch fresh dill, finely chopped
3 tablespoons walnuts, crushed
2 tablespoons olive or sunflower oil
Salt, if desired

Mix yogurt and water in a large bowl. Add cucmber, garlic, dill, walnuts, and oil. Stir to mix. Salt to taste. Place in the fridge to chill for an hour.

MONASTERY *GYUVETCH*

This dish was traditionally served in the famous Rila Monastery. It is simple and filling.

2 pounds beef, cut into cubes
Olive oil
4 tomatoes, chopped
½ pound mushrooms
1 cup rice
1 onion, chopped
15 whole olives
Fresh parsley
2 tablespoons vegetable oil
1 tablespoon butter
1 tablespoon sugar
2½ cups beef stock or broth
Black pepper, paprika, and salt to taste

Fry the beef in a pan with the olive oil until brown, about 5 minutes. Add the onion, beef stock, and paprika. After a few minutes, add the mushrooms and rice. Simmer for about 15 minutes. Add tomatoes, salt, butter, sugar, and olives, and cook for another 5 minutes. Preheat oven to 400°F. Transfer the contents of the pan to a baking dish and bake in the oven for 30 minutes. Sprinkle with parsley and pepper before serving.

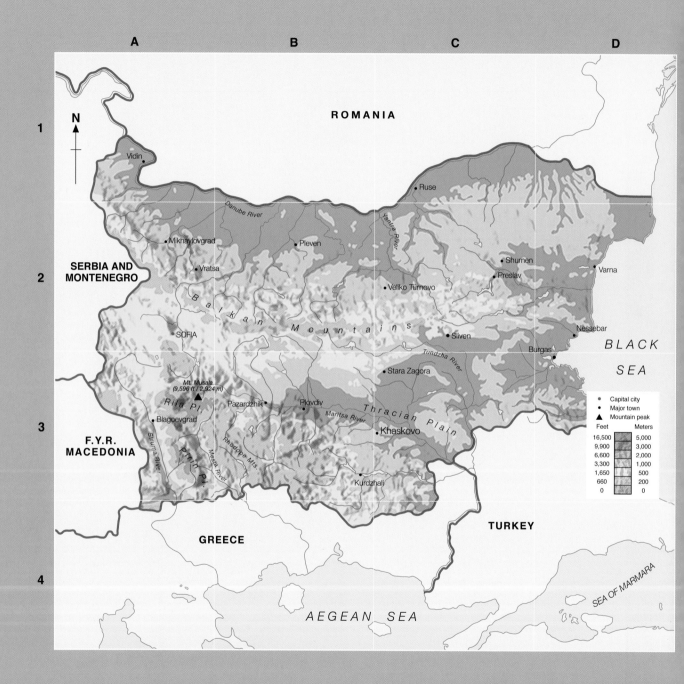

A　　　　　**B**　　　　　**C**　　　　　**D**

ROMANIA

1

N

Vidin

Ruse

**SERBIA AND
MONTENEGRO**

Danube River

Mikhaylovgrad

Pleven

Yantra River

Shumen

Vratsa

Preslav

Varna

2

Balkan

Mountains

Veliko Turnovo

SOFIA

Sliven

Nessebar

Tundzha River

Burgas

BLACK

SEA

Mt. Musala
(9,596 ft / 2,924 m)

Stara Zagora

Rila Pl.

Pazardzhik

Plovdiv

Thracian Plain

**F.Y.R.
MACEDONIA**

Blagoevgrad

Maritsa River

Khaskovo

Struma River

Pirin Pl.

Rhodope Mts.

Mesta River

3

Kurdzhali

TURKEY

GREECE

	Capital city
	Major town
▲	Mountain peak

Feet		Meters
16,500		5,000
9,900		3,000
6,600		2,000
3,300		1,000
1,650		500
660		200
0		0

4

SEA OF MARMARA

AEGEAN   SEA

MAP OF BULGARIA

ECONOMIC BULGARIA

Manufacturing

 Electronics

 Metal Products

 Textiles

Services

 Airport

 Port

 Tourism

Natural Resources

 Fish

Oil Processing

 Rose Oil

Timber

Agriculture

 Cattle

 Corn

 Grapes

Tobacco

 Wheat

ABOUT THE ECONOMY

OVERVIEW

Bulgaria, a former Communist country, entered the European Union on January 1, 2007, although as of 2016 it had not yet met the requirements to adopt the euro as a form of currency. Bulgaria has experienced economic stability and strong growth since 1996, when a major economic downturn led to the collapse of the socialist government. As a result, the government implemented economic reforms and responsible fiscal planning. Low inflation and steady progress on structural reforms have improved the business environment. Following a sharp downturn in 2008 and 2009 due to the global financial crisis, Bulgaria's economy has seen slow but steady growth, reaching an annual growth rate of about 3 percent in 2016. The country has attracted significant amounts of direct foreign investment.

GROSS DOMESTIC PRODUCT

$47.17 billion (2015)

GDP BY SECTOR

Services 67.2 percent; industry 27.6 percent; agriculture 5.1 percent (2016)

CURRENCY

1 lev (BGN) = 100 stotinki
Notes: 2, 5, 10, 20, 50, 100 leva
Coins: 1, 2, 5, 10, 20, 50 stotinki; 1 lev
1 USD = 1.75 BGN (November 2016)

NATURAL RESOURCES

Bauxite, copper, lead, zinc, coal, timber.

AGRICULTURAL PRODUCTS

Vegetables, fruits, tobacco, wine, wheat, barley, sunflowers, sugar beets, livestock, dairy products.

MAJOR EXPORTS

Clothing and footwear; iron and steel; machinery and equipment; fuels.

MAJOR IMPORTS

Machinery and equipment; metals and ores; chemicals and plastics; fuels and raw materials.

MAJOR TRADING PARTNERS

Italy, Russia, Turkey, Germany, Greece, Belgium, France.

WORKFORCE

2.5 million (2015)

WORKFORCE BY SECTOR

Services 62.8 percent; industry 30.3 percent; agriculture 6.9 percent (2014)

UNEMPLOYMENT RATE

10.1 percent (2015)

INFLATION RATE

—1.1 percent (2015)

CULTURAL BULGARIA

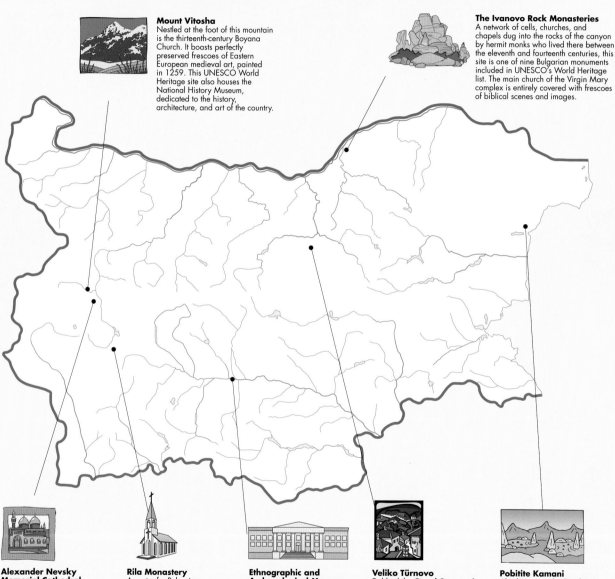

Mount Vitosha
Nestled at the foot of this mountain is the thirteenth-century Boyana Church. It boasts perfectly preserved frescoes of Eastern European medieval art, painted in 1259. This UNESCO World Heritage site also houses the National History Museum, dedicated to the history, architecture, and art of the country.

The Ivanovo Rock Monasteries
A network of cells, churches, and chapels dug into the rocks of the canyon by hermit monks who lived there between the eleventh and fourteenth centuries, this site is one of nine Bulgarian monuments included in UNESCO's World Heritage list. The main church of the Virgin Mary complex is entirely covered with frescoes of biblical scenes and images.

Alexander Nevsky Memorial Cathedral
Built in 1912 to honor the two hundred thousand Russians who died in the Russian-Turkish Liberation War, which brought independence to Bulgaria, this is a lavish example of neo-Byzantine architecture. Its museum houses over three hundred icon paintings and murals, some a thousand years old.

Rila Monastery
A center for Bulgarian spiritual and cultural life during the five-hundred-year Turkish occupation, this tenth-century monastery has been a UNESCO-listed World Heritage site since 1983. It is famous for its wall paintings by Zakhari Zograph, intricate carvings such as the Raphael's Cross, and valuable icons painted between the fourteenth and nineteenth centuries.

Ethnographic and Archaeological Museum
Founded in 432 BCE, Plovdiv has many archaeological treasures, including a Roman theater and stadium, ancient fortifications, and Nebet Tepe, a prehistoric settlement. The Ethnographic Museum has lavish displays of locally produced textiles, pottery, and other crafts, while the Archaeological Museum is devoted to Thracian culture and artifacts from as far back as 4000 BCE.

Veliko Türnovo
Dubbed the City of Czars and the "second Constantinople," this was Bulgaria's capital from the twelfth to fourteenth centuries. Situated high above winding river gorges, the town's historic attractions include the Tsarevets Fortress, the sixteenth-century Church of the Nativity, and the ruins of the Samovodska Charshia complex. In summer the town lights up with a spectacular sound-and-light show.

Pobitite Kamani
Also known as the Fossil Forest, this unique geological site was formed over a period of fifty-one to fifty-three million years ago, and was home to the Mesolithic Middle Stone Age tribes. There, hundreds of stone pillars rise from the earth, some up to 32 feet (10 m) high, spanning an area of 27 square miles (70 sq km).

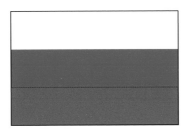

OFFICIAL NAME
Republic of Bulgaria

FLAG DESCRIPTION
Three equal horizontal bands of white
(top), green (middle), and red (bottom)

CAPITAL
Sofia

OTHER MAJOR CITIES
Plovdiv, Varna, Burgas, Ruse, Stara Zagora,
Pleven, and Sliven (in order of population)

INDEPENDENCE DAY
March 3, 1878 (autonomous within
    Ottoman Empire)
September 22, 1908 (from the
    Ottoman Empire)

ETHNIC GROUPS
Bulgarians 76.9 percent, unknown 10
percent, Turks 8 percent, Roma 4.4
percent, others less than 1 percent

RELIGIOUS GROUPS
Bulgarian Orthodox 59.4 percent, Muslim
7.8 percent, no religion 27.4 percent,
atheist 3.7, others (including Roman
Catholic, Protestant, and Jews) less
than 1 percent

BIRTHRATE
8.8 births per 1,000 Bulgarians (2016)

DEATH RATE
14.5 deaths per 1,000 Bulgarians (2016)

MAIN LANGUAGES
Bulgarian (76.8 percent) is the official
language and the Cyrillic alphabet is used.
Minority languages include Turkish
(8.2 percent), Roma (3.8 percent), and
others (0.7 percent).

LITERACY RATE
People ages fifteen and above who can read
and write: 98.4 percent (2015)

LEADERS IN POLITICS
Todor Zhivkov (1911—1998), Bulgaria's
    Communist dictator from 1954 to 1989.
Petar Mladenov, first president of the
    Republic of Bulgaria in 1990.
Zheliu Zhelev, president from 1990 to 1997.
Petar Stoyanov, president from 1997 to 2002.
Georgi Parvanov, president from 2002
    to 2012.
Angel Marin, vice-president from 2002
    to 2012.
Sergei Stanishev, prime minister from 2005
    to 2009.
Margarita Popova, vice president from 2012
    to 2017.
Boyko Borisov, prime minister from 2009 to
    2013 and 2014 to 2016.
Rumen Radev, current president since 2017.

TIMELINE

IN BULGARIA	IN THE WORLD
	600 CE
681	Height of Mayan civilization.
First Bulgarian Kingdom.	
1018–1185	
Byzantine rule.	
1352	
Beginning of rule by Ottoman Empire.	**1789–1799**
March 3, 1878	The French Revolution.
Liberation from Ottoman rule.	**1914**
1919	World War I begins.
Bulgarian Communist Party (BCP) founded.	**1939**
1943	World War II begins.
Bulgaria's King Boris returns from a meeting with Hitler and dies mysteriously.	
1944	
Soviet army invades German-occupied Bulgaria. Soviet-backed Fatherland Front assumes power.	
1946	
Bulgaria's monarchy abolished. Communist Party wins election. Georgi Dimitrov elected prime minister.	
1947	
A new constitution along Soviet lines establishes one-party state. The economy and industrial sectors are nationalized.	**1949**
	The North Atlantic Treaty Organization (NATO) is formed.
	1957
	The Russians launch *Sputnik 1*.
	1966–1969
1971	The Chinese Cultural Revolution.
Todor Zhivkov becomes president of Bulgaria.	
1984	
Zhivkov government forces Turkish minority to take Slavic names.	**1986**
	Nuclear power disaster at Chernobyl in Ukraine.

IN BULGARIA	IN THE WORLD
1989	
Mass exodus of Bulgarian Turks. Foreign Minister Petar Mladenov ousts Zhivkov. Union of Democratic Forces (UDF) formed.	
1990	
Economic crisis. Communist Party becomes the Bulgarian Socialist Party (BSP). UDF's Zheliu Zhelev becomes president.	
1991	**1991**
UDF wins election.	Breakup of the Soviet Union.
1994	
BSP returns to power in general election.	
1997	**1997**
Mass protests over economic crisis. UDF leader Ivan Kostov becomes prime minister.	Hong Kong is returned to China..
2001	**2001**
Socialist Party leader Georgi Parvanov becomes president.	Terrorists crash planes in New York, Washington, DC, and Pennsylvania.
2002	
Bulgaria formally invited to join NATO at the Prague Summit.	**2003**
	War in Iraq begins.
2004	
Bulgaria is admitted to NATO.	
2005	
Bulgaria signs EU accession treaty and implements economic reforms.	
2007	
Bulgaria admitted to EU January 1.	**2009**
	Barack Obama becomes the first African American president of the United States.
2015	**2015**
Bulgaria extends its fence along the border with Turkey to stop the flow of illegal immigrants from the Middle East.	Dozens are killed in terrorist attacks in Paris carried out by ISIS.
2016	**2016**
Bulgaria holds presidential elections. Rumen Radev elected. Prime Minister Boyko Borisov announces resignation.	Donald Trump elected president of the United States.

GLOSSARY

atheist
A person who does not believe in God or other deities.

bolyar (or boyar) (BOH-lyahr)
A Bulgarian feudal lord.

Bulgars (BOOL-gahrs)
A nomadic tribe of Turanian origin, which formed a coalition with the Balkan Slavs and founded the Bulgarian state in 681 CE.

chorbadjia **(chor-BAHD-ji-ya)**
The richest Bulgarian in a village of the nineteenth century, often a collaborator of the local Turkish government.

Cyrillic (ser-IL-lik)
Based on the alphabet created by Saints Cyril and Methodius and used for the writing of the Slavic languages.

excavate
To dig something out of the ground, especially an artifact or an object from ancient times.

haidouk **(hai-DOOK)**
A member of the spontaneous underground movement against the Ottoman government, which started in the last decade of the fourteenth century.

horo **(ho-RO)**
A lively circular folk dance of many of the Balkan peoples.

Ignazhden
A festival on December 20 marking the first day of the Christmas holidays.

Nestinari (nays-ti-NAH-ri)
People with the gift of dancing on red-hot embers on May 21, Saints Constantine and Helena Day.

patriarch
The head of one of the Eastern Orthodox churches, such as the Bulgarian Church.

perestroika (per-ah-STROY-kah)
Literally, "reformation." The transformation of the Communist economic and political system into a free-market democracy.

rakia **(rah-KI-yah)**
A Bulgarian grape or plum brandy popular as an aperitif.

survaki **(SOOR-vah-ki) (or** *survakane***)**
A tradition observed on New Year's Day, when children visit their elders and family friends to wish them health and prosperity.

FOR FURTHER INFORMATION

BOOKS

Bousfield, Jonathan, and Matt Willis. *DK Eyewitness Travel Guide: Bulgaria*. New York: Eyewitness Travel, 2014.

Forbes, Nevill. *The Balkans: A History of Bulgaria and Serbia*. Seattle, WA: Create Space Independent Publishing, 2015.

Konstantinov, Aleko. *Bai Ganyo: Incredible Tales of a Modern Bulgarian*. Madison, WI: University of Wisconsin Press, 2010.

Kostova, Elizabeth. *The Shadow Land*. New York: Ballantine Books, 2017.

Tzvetkova, Julianna. *Bulgaria—Culture Smart! The Essential Guide to Customs and Culture*. London, UK: Kuperard, 2015.

WEBSITES

Central Intelligence Agency World Factbook: Bulgaria
https://www.cia.gov/library/publications/the-world-factbook/geos/bu.html
Every Culture: Bulgaria
http://www.everyculture.com/Bo-Co/Bulgaria.html
Go East Europe
http://goeasteurope.about.com/od/bulgariaandthebalkans/ss/bulgariaculture.htm

FILMS

Eastern Plays/Iztochni piesi. Waterfront Films, 2009.

The Judgement/Sadilshteto. Premium Films, 2014.

The World is Big and Salvation Lurks Around the Corner/Svetat e golyam I spasenie debne otvsyakade. RFF International, 2008.

BIBLIOGRAPHY

Baker, Mark. *Romania and Bulgaria*. Footscray, Australia: Lonely Planet Publications, 2013.

Bousfield, Jonathan, and Matt Willis. *DK Eyewitness Travel Guide: Bulgaria*. New York: Eyewitness Travel, 2014.

Chary, Frederick B. *The History of Bulgaria*. Santa Barbara, CA: Greenwood Press, 2011.

DK Publishing. *Bulgaria*. New York: DK Publishing, Inc., 2012.

Forbes, Nevill. *The Balkans: A History of Bulgaria and Serbia*. Seattle, WA: Create Space Independent Publishing, 2015.

Konstantinov, Aleko. *Bai Ganyo: Incredible Tales of a Modern Bulgarian*. Madison, WI: University of Wisconsin Press, 2010.

Kostova, Elizabeth. *The Shadow Land*. New York: Ballantine Books, 2017.

Rosendo, Joseph. *Travel Scope*, Season 8, Episode 15: "Hungary, Croatia, Serbia, Bulgaria, and Romania: Eastern European Treasures." Topanga, CA: Travelscope LLC, 2015.

Tzvetkova, Julianna. *Bulgaria—Culture Smart! The Essential Guide to Customs and Culture*. London, UK: Kuperard, 2015.

INDEX

INDEX